Contents

CHILDREN'S NUTRITION

A Parent's Guide

Need
— 2 —
Know

**Angela Falaschi
& Andréa Childs**

Children's Nutrition – A Parent's Guide is also available in accessible formats for people with any degree of sight loss. The large print edition and ebook (with accessibility features enabled) are available from Need2Know. Please let us know if there are any special features you require and we will do our best to accommodate your needs.

First published in Great Britain in 2011 by
Need2Know
Remus House
Coltsfoot Drive
Peterborough
PE2 9JX
Telephone 01733 898103
Fax 01733 313524
www.need2knowbooks.co.uk

Need2Know is an imprint of Bonacia Ltd.
www.forwardpoetry.co.uk
SB ISBN 978-1-86144-117-1
Cover photograph: Dreamstime

Introduction

We decided to write this book because many parents are confused about the best foods to buy and how to encourage their children to eat them. This is despite childhood nutrition being hotly debated by the government, health organisations, food manufacturers and the media. Our aim is not to dictate rules, but to be a helping hand for anyone wanting to make the best food choices for their family.

Every family, each parent and child, is unique – physically, emotionally and financially. But the nutrients required by the body from childhood to adulthood remain the same. Each generation changes but the results of good nutrition do not. This book is for parents, grandparents, carers and teachers of children aged from zero to 18. It offers a comprehensive guide to the building blocks of a healthy diet, plus recipes that can be enjoyed by all the family.

There is a greater choice of items than ever on our supermarket shelves, and we can buy a huge range of organic goods and browse for locally-grown produce at farmers' markets. But not all progress has been positive. Convenience meals, jars of baby food and takeaways offer a quick fix for time-poor parents and their children, but intensive farming practices and modern food preparation and preservation techniques mean that they can be inferior in nutritional value.

So what does this mean for our children? Despite the reassuring face of a smiling cherub on the packaging of a bought baby purée or ready meals marketed at children, we believe these foods should be emergency standbys, not the basis of a child's diet. Food and lifestyles may be different from when we were children, but the health of our young ones is different too, with allergies, obesity, hyperactivity and other problems increasing year by year. Growing children (and their parents) should eat naturally prepared and simply cooked foods that are fresh, local and in season. Home-made meals like this don't have to be expensive – in fact, this book proves it's possible to eat well on a relatively small budget, an important consideration in today's economic climate.

Nutritionist Angela Falaschi, and writer Andréa Childs, who is a mother of two young children, present real-life case studies, and parent-friendly advice on how to choose, prepare, cook – and most importantly – enjoy food as a family. Many of the recipes have an Italian flavour, inspired by Angela's childhood in Italy and the meals she grew up with. Since then, scientists have proven that the traditional Mediterranean diet provides a superb balance of nutrients that helps to promote wellbeing for life. We hope this book will inspire you to make positive, delicious changes to your family's diet.

Note

All names of case studies have been changed in order to protect individuals' identities.

Disclaimer

This book is for general information on childhood nutrition and isn't intended to replace professional medical advice. It can be used alongside professional medical advice but anyone thinking about introducing changes to their child's diet and lifestyle is strongly advised to consult their child's healthcare professional first.

Chapter One

Good Food for Children

Why diet is so important for children

Every stage of a child's development makes fresh demands on their body – they need bone-building calcium for growth spurts; essential fatty acids for an evolving brain; and vitamins to boost immunity. That's why a good diet is so essential to keep children healthy, strong, alert and happy.

However, it's more important than that. Researchers have shown that good nutrition in the early years can give a child the best chance of a long and healthy adulthood, reducing their risk of developing conditions such as heart disease, obesity, diabetes and cancer.

It works the other way round, too. Giving your child foods that are high in saturated fat, salt and sugar can increase their risk of poor health, both now and when they grow up. It also means they fail to develop a taste for healthy options, and don't learn about how fantastic good food can make them feel.

Whether you're a parent, carer, playgroup leader or teacher, providing healthy meals and teaching what makes a good diet is one of the ways you can protect and support the children you look after. Thankfully, the importance of good nutrition and the pleasure of cooking, eating and sharing food are now promoted more widely in newspapers and magazines, by the government, health authorities and in schools. Unfortunately, there is also a lot of confusion about what 'healthy' food actually is. This book will show you that it doesn't have to be difficult, or expensive, to create meals that children love, that help them to develop a strong immune system and provide all the nutrients their growing bodies need.

'A good diet cannot guarantee good health for our children – but it is a vital first step.'

Time pressures and quick-fix diets

No one should underestimate the immense pressure that parents, carers, schools and nurseries face today. When you're juggling a job, home life, budget and the demands of families and individuals, it's all too easy to take short cuts and that can mean substituting home-cooked food for ready meals, takeaways and cheap and easy (but not always nutritious) options at the dinner table. But as parents and carers we are also acutely aware that what children eat is essential for their health and happiness. Here are a few tips to help you keep your good intentions, so that you can shop, cook and eat in a way that's tasty, healthy and affordable, and won't have you slaving for hours in front of the cooker!

■ Plan meals in advance, write down what you need to buy, and stick to your shopping list. This will save you time and money at the supermarket, and means you won't order an expensive and greasy pizza because you've nothing in the fridge for dinner!

■ Keep a list of 20 or so favourite family meals and use them to plan weekly menus, swapping the mix around each time. Try to add in one new recipe each week, so you can introduce different nutrients and flavours.

■ If you can, do a basic weekly or fortnightly shop, but buy fruit and vegetables every few days to ensure they're as fresh as possible.

■ Prepare lunch boxes the night before to cut down on the morning rush, leaving time for you and your child to enjoy a healthy breakfast.

■ Prepare double portions of casseroles, soups and sauces, or dishes like lasagne, so you can freeze one for another time.

■ Take advantage of late-night and Sunday opening at supermarkets – you will be able to think more clearly when the store is less busy, and take advantage of the price reductions on food at the end of the day or weekend.

Need2Know

The problem of poor diet

When eating and cooking is just a chore, it's not only the pleasure of sharing meals or the joy of tasting delicious food that is lost. Many families eat the same limited number of foods week in and week out, and that can create nutritional imbalances that can be damaging for children and the adults that care for them. This can be a problem even with fresh, home-cooked food, but when meals are too often derived from heavily processed ingredients or come ready-made from the fridge or freezer, the implications for a child's health are even greater. The risk of allergies, obesity, infections, skin conditions and juvenile-onset diabetes may be increased by a poor diet.

Food manufacturers use preservatives, flavourings, emulsifiers, stabilisers and thickeners to make their products appeal to our eyes and taste buds, so we (especially children) crave these unhealthy options more. These additives also increase the shelf life of foods and the profit margins of the companies that produce them. Some health professionals have raised questions about the long-term safety of food additives, as well as their immediate impact on child health and behaviour.

'According to recent studies, foods high in salt, fat and sugar can cause changes in your child's brain chemistry that make them crave these foods more.'

Food-related ailments

As well as general health problems, there can be links between what a child eats and specific ailments. Even a healthy diet can trigger a reaction if a child is sensitive to a certain food. Knowing how to identify and manage these triggers is a major step to ensuring your child's good health.

Allergies

There has been an explosion in recent years in the number of children suffering food allergies. But there has also been a rise in other allergic conditions, such as hay fever, asthma and eczema. While scientists are unsure about some of the reasons for these rises, it is known that having a close family member who suffers from an allergy, including food allergies, hay fever, eczema and asthma, increases a child's risk of developing an allergic condition, although it might be different to that suffered by their parents or siblings.

- If you think your child is at risk from allergies, or you are concerned about feeding them safely, speak to your GP, health visitor or an allergy specialist.

- Common allergens include milk, eggs, nuts, fruit, soya, wheat, fish and shellfish.

- If you know you are allergic to a certain food, give a small amount to your child, unmixed with other foods, so you can monitor for any reaction.

- Make sure an allergic child's diet is rich in vitamin C, essential fatty acids (if fish is not the problem), beta carotene (which the body converts into vitamin A), magnesium (important for muscles, nerves and the metabolism of calcium), calcium (for strong bones and teeth) and zinc (essential for growth and development).

Food sensitivity

Your child does not need to have an allergy in order to be sensitive to certain foods. Food sensitivity or intolerance can cause stomach pains, bloating, excess wind, constipation and diarrhoea, and contribute to conditions such as eczema, asthma and hay fever.

It is often the case that tracking down which food or foods trigger the reaction and removing them from the diet for a period will help to eliminate these symptoms. Common problem foods include yeast, cow's milk, cheese, seeds, eggs, gluten (found in wheat and rye), corn, soya products (such as tofu and tempeh), peppers and aubergines. For that reason, you may want to restrict these foods until your child is around one year old, and to introduce them into their diet gradually in order to monitor for any problems.

Food intolerances can develop when a food is eaten in large amounts. For example, a child may begin to react to wheat if they have toast for breakfast, sandwiches for lunch and pasta for dinner every day.

If you suspect your child may be intolerant to a certain food, keep a food diary of what they eat for a week. Keep a three-day gap before eating the same food again (except for fruit and vegetables, unless you have noticed that your child has a problem with them). The gap will help you to discover if your child has a delayed reaction to eating a certain food. For more advice about food intolerances, consult your GP or a nutritionist.

Obesity

Childhood obesity is increasing but amid all the sensational headlines, government warnings and food industry advertising, it can be hard for a concerned parent or carer to know whether a child's dimples are baby fat or a sign that they're overweight. If you are concerned about your child's weight, the first step is to get a proper assessment from a GP or health professional. This will look at their body fat percentage in relation to their age and height, and may also investigate if there is an underlying health problem.

It's also worth looking at your child's (and the family's) lifestyle – how much sugary, fatty, or processed foods do they eat? Do they regularly have five portions of fruit and vegetables per day? What activities are they involved in? Making joint decisions about the foods you eat can be a good way to explain the importance of a good diet and to involve your child in making healthier food choices. Planning activities as a family, such as bike rides, sport activities, or just games in the park, can also boost fitness levels for you and your child, helping to overcome any weight problems. Read more about obesity in chapter 6.

'Making joint decisions about the foods you eat can be a good way to explain the importance of a good diet and to involve your child in making healthier food choices.'

Quick tip

Check food labels for added sugar, salt, additives and saturated fats. Generally, the shorter the ingredient list the healthier the food.

Eating well on a budget

It's easy to be seduced by cheap deals on processed foods at the shops, but feeding the family tasty, healthy meals doesn't have to cost more. It is true that the prices of certain foods, such as fresh fruit and vegetables, can seem expensive and that many people (and organisations such as schools and nurseries) have recently had to reduce their spending, meaning they can't afford to buy the food they would prefer for the children in their care. But it is possible to spend less and still eat well.

- Cut out unhealthy choices like chips, crisps, chocolate, fast food, burgers and fizzy drinks, which leave you hungry and wanting more, and you'll be amazed at the money you save – not to mention the improvement in your child's physical, mental and emotional wellbeing.

- Remember that babies and toddlers generally eat what they are given and enjoy even bland flavours. This is the time to introduce healthy foods such as home-made vegetable and fruit purées, which cost a lot less than manufactured baby food and children's ready meals.

- Plan your menu each week, so you are in control of your food budget.

- Eat low-cost vegetarian meals such as baked potatoes, delicious home-made soups and tasty bean casseroles, as well as more expensive meat and fish dishes.

- Think about how you can extend meals. The remains of a roast chicken, for example, could make a delicious stir-fry or salad, or you could serve a basic tomato sauce with pasta one day and home-made pizza the next.

- Take advantage of 2 for 1 deals on foods like fresh berries – eat one punnet and freeze the other so you always have the ingredients for a vitamin-packed smoothie to hand.

- Grow your own herbs and vegetables – they will cost a fraction of shop prices, and watching where food comes from and helping it to grow will encourage your child to eat their harvest.

- Sprouting is also fun for children – seeds and pulses will grow very quickly sown on damp paper. Try sunflower, pumpkin, alfalfa or mung beans. Give them to your child as a nutrient-packed snack or sprinkle them into salads.

- Don't shop on an empty stomach, you'll end up buying more than you need.

'The fresher your fruit and vegetables, the more nutrients they will contain.'

Fresh and seasonal is best

The fresher your fruit and vegetables, the more nutrients they will contain – there's no better way for your child to get the vitamins and minerals, fibre and carbohydrates they need. Eating foods in the season they would naturally develop, rather than produce that has been grown in an artificial environment so it can appear in the shops all year round, is another guarantee of flavour and quality. It's far better to eat strawberries that are grown in Britain in the summertime, fed by natural sunshine, soil and rainwater, than those that are flown thousands of food miles in the winter, nurtured under artificial light and in heated polytunnels and fed with artificial fertilisers.

Eating seasonally will also teach your child about the rhythm of the natural world and how our bodies have developed in tune with it – it's no coincidence that the hedgerows are full of blackberries that are rich in vitamin C just as our bodies are preparing for autumn; that starchy vegetables thrive in winter when we need their comforting energy; or that fresh salads appear in the summer when we crave light and fresh raw foods.

When buying fresh produce, always choose shops where the stock moves fast, so you can be sure the food has not been there a long time. Supermarkets and good greengrocers should have a fast turnover of fresh food, but check that the fruit and vegetables you choose aren't limp, bruised or tired looking – all signs they've been out of the fields and on the shelves too long. Local and farmers' markets are a great way to buy fresh at a reasonable price, and your child will love the colour and bustle of the stalls.

It's a brilliant idea to get your child involved when buying fruit and vegetables – ask them to find all the colours of the rainbow to bring home in their basket, as the different colours of fresh produce indicate the varying nutrients they contain.

Frozen produce

Frozen vegetables and fruit can save busy parents time and money, especially as the speed with which they are picked and packaged helps to preserve vital nutrients. Keep a few bags in the freezer for those days when the fruit basket and vegetable box are bare.

Going organic

The price of organic foods has fallen as both supply and demand have increased, but they still tend to be more expensive than non-organic options. The benefits of eating organic for your child are that organic foods generally contain more nutrients than intensively cultivated foods, and they are free from the growth hormones, pesticides and other chemicals used in conventional farming. For example, an apple that has been naturally ripened will have a higher vitamin content than a non-organic one that has been sprayed with fungicides and insecticides, and harvested early before it is fully ripe so that it can be transported when it is less likely to bruise.

'The benefits of eating organic for your child are that organic foods generally contain more nutrients than intensively cultivated foods.'

It may not be possible to give your child a totally organic diet, but buying some naturally produced meat, fruit, vegetables and dairy products is a great start. Even if buying organic isn't an option, serving your child a good range of fresh foods is one of the most important steps you can make for their health, now and in the future.

Food and families

What we eat feeds our bodies, but how we eat it nurtures our heart and soul. Involve your child in buying, preparing and cooking the food you serve and you will be amazed at how their taste for healthy and delicious natural flavours develops. There's no better way to get your child to try new foods and to be sure they eat their meals – without arguments! It's essential that mealtimes do not become battlegrounds. If your child refuses the meal you have prepared, do not force them to eat it. It's better to remove the dish and try preparing and serving the food in a different way next time.

Sitting down at the table together will encourage your child to explore the tastes and textures of different foods, as they seek to eat what the grown-ups do. Eating with family and friends will also encourage your child to socialise and provide happy memories of time with loved ones – celebrations wouldn't be the same without the food we share. Your child will remember the conversations around the dinner table, not a television programme that was on in the background. Switch off the TV and enjoy this time together.

Summing Up

- What you feed your child can establish eating patterns for life.

- A well-balanced diet that is rich in nutrients can help to prevent health problems in both childhood and adulthood.

- Diets that are high in artificial additives, processed foods, salt, sugar and saturated fats can cause health problems for your child now and in the future.

- Planning healthy meals in advance can save you time, stress and money.

- Fresh, seasonal foods should have priority in your shopping basket.

- Involving your child in planning and cooking meals can encourage healthy eating.

- Eating with family and friends can create positive associations with food for your child.

Chapter Two

Essential Nutrition

Nutrients can be divided into six major categories: carbohydrates, proteins, fats, vitamins, minerals and water. Together, they work like a football team, each providing essential qualities that lead towards one goal – good health.

- The nutrients that we need daily in fairly large amounts are carbohydrates, proteins, fats and water. These are known as macronutrients.
- The nutrients that we need in smaller quantities, such as vitamins, minerals and trace minerals, are called micronutrients.

Macronutrients

Carbohydrates

Carbohydrates are found in grains such as, wheat and rice; pasta; cakes and pastries; pulses, including beans, lentils and peas; some root vegetables; sugar and honey. Carbohydrates are broken down by the body into a sugar called glucose, providing the fuel that your child needs for a day of growing, playing and learning.

Simple carbohydrates

- Simple carbohydrates are easily digested, leading to a rapid rise in the amount of glucose in your child's blood. The energy contained in simple carbohydrates is quickly released, but it is also quickly used up and your child will soon feel hungry again.

- White flour is used to make white bread, cakes and pastries. As well as reducing the nutrient content of flour, the refining process cuts down on the amount of fibre and creates easily digestible 'double sugars', making these foods easy to digest and creating a surge of sugar in the body after eating.

- In time, high consumption of refined carbohydrates, especially sucrose (white sugar) can lead to poor health.

Quick tip

It's generally best to avoid giving too many simple carbohydrates to your child, but a snack like a biscuit or fruit smoothie, which release energy quickly, can be just the between-meals boost they need after sport or playtime at the park.

'Very few children don't like pasta. Choose wholegrain varieties which are rich in B vitamins, and their bodies will love it too.'

Complex carbohydrates

These are made from long chains of sugar (polysaccharides) that are digested slowly, so energy is released at a more steady pace and lasts for a longer period of time. Complex carbohydrates are found in wholegrains, wholemeal flour, wild rice, whole oats, pulses and some vegetables. Complex carbohydrates are full of nutrients, and the fibre they contain will help your child to feel fuller for longer after meals and so prevent overeating.

Good grains

Here in the UK (and the West generally) we eat a diet that is rich in wheat, but there are lots more wholegrains that can provide different nutrients and flavours for your child.

- Buckwheat – this is actually a seed, but it has all the goodness of wholegrain and it can be used as an alternative to wholegrain flour. High in fibre, rutin (a naturally occurring plant chemical with antioxidant and anti-inflammatory properties), magnesium and B vitamins. Try it in noodles or home-made pancakes.

Need2Know

- Corn – rich in some B vitamins, high in fibre, beta carotene and vitamin C. Home-made popcorn, popped without oil, is a great alternative to crisps for your child.

- Quinoa – now easily and cheaply available from supermarkets. Quinoa is a good source of fibre and B vitamins. Unlike wheat it's free from gluten, which can upset the digestion of those sensitive to it. Serve it as an alternative to rice.

Proteins

Proteins are like building blocks, essential for the growth and repair of every single cell in your child's body. Protein requirements rise during periods of fast growth, including infancy, so it's essential that your child eats at least two portions of protein each day.

- Protein foods are digested by specific acids in the stomach and are broken down into smaller units called amino acids.

- Around 20 amino acids are required by the body to make the various types of protein. Eight of these amino acids (nine in children) must be supplied by the diet. These are known as essential amino acids.

- It's important that your child eats sufficient protein-rich foods, such as meat, poultry, fish, milk, cheese, eggs, soya products, nuts and seeds.

- The body cannot store proteins. Excess amounts are converted into energy and fat.

Getting the protein balance right

Proteins from animal sources contain all of the nine essential amino acids and are called 'complete' proteins. Plants foods lack some amino acids and are therefore called 'incomplete'. It's important that your child eats a variety of protein foods. Vegetarians and vegans must select foods that complement one another and eat them in the same meal in order to obtain all of the essential amino acids they need.

Certain food combinations complement each other, providing a mix of essential amino acids as well as the perfect balance of flavours in a meal. For example, legumes such as beans are deficient in the amino acids methionine

'Give protein and carbohydrates together in the same meal. Fibre from the carbohydrates will aid digestion, and the protein will help energy to be released more slowly and last longer, so your child won't feel hungry soon after eating.'

and cysteine, but rich in lysine. Grains, seeds and nuts are rich in cysteine and methionine, but lacking in lysine. If you combine these two types of foods, for example, in a vegetable chilli with kidney beans and rice, they will provide all the essential amino acids your child needs. Your child's other meals throughout the day will compliment these, providing a balanced diet.

Case study: the vegetarian child

Jenny brought her three-year-old daughter to see me because she was underweight and prone to skin infections. Both mother and daughter followed a vegetarian diet and after asking Jenny to keep a diary of what foods Lisa was eating, I realised the little girl's diet was lacking in protein – she ate mainly pizza, pasta and white bread sandwiches.

I explained to Jenny that it was important to cut down on the amount of refined carbohydrates her daughter was eating, as they were creating an imbalance in her intestinal flora that was contributing to her pimples and suppressing her appetite for other foods. I suggested she eat fruit, such as mango and papaya, which boosts skin health.

As Jenny and her daughter didn't eat meat or fish, it was important that they chose foods that would combine on the plate to provide complete proteins – I recommended soya beans, wholegrains, nuts, seeds and wheatgerm. It's advisable for vegetarian children to eat some milk, eggs or cheese to complement the missing proteins in plants. Other good combinations are: grains and legumes, which supplement each other's missing amino acids; hummus is also a complete protein, due to its combination of chickpeas and sesame seeds; peanut butter on wholegrain toast; and rice with lentils or tofu.

Jenny returned six weeks later. Her daughter had put on 2kg and her skin was much clearer.

'White and oily fish are great sources of protein, making them particularly nutritious foods for children.'

Fats

Many parents and carers are concerned about the amount of fat that their children eat, but fat is actually essential for the health of your child's body.

- Fat provides high energy, insulation and protects the internal organs.

- It helps to form cells and membranes that are essential to the function of the nervous system.

- It transports vitamins A, E, D and K around the body.

- It helps to regulate enzymes (substances that perform specific chemical reactions, such as breaking down food and building up bones) and produce prostaglandins (hormone-like substances that are essential for many body processes).

- Fat also helps to make our food more palatable.

Of course, a diet of chips and chocolate isn't going to lead to good health, what's more important is the type of fat your child eats.

- Saturated fats are found in animal products such as meat, milk and butter. They have been linked to obesity and conditions such as heart disease, and should be eaten in small quantities.

- Polyunsaturated fats come from vegetable sources, such as plant oils, nuts and seeds. These provide vital nutrients called essential fatty acids, essential because the body cannot make them itself.

Essential fatty acids

There are two types of essential fatty acids – omega 6 (also known as linoleic acid or LA) and omega 3 (also known as linolenic acid or LNA). These types of fat are good for building the body's cells, especially those of the brain and nervous system – essential in a developing child.

- Omega 6 – good sources are hemp, pumpkin seeds, sunflower oil, safflower oil, corn, soya bean and wheatgerm. Safflower is the richest source of omega 6.

- Omega 3 – good sources include oily fish such as herring, salmon, sardines and fresh tuna, as well as flaxseed (also known as linseed). Flaxseeds contain the most omega 3.

Case study: siblings with asthma

Amanda came to me to make sure that her four children, aged two, four, seven and 12, were eating a balanced diet. The two oldest children had acne and also suffered from asthma, which ran in the family.

The children's diet, particularly that of the two eldest, was too high in dairy products – they loved processed cheese sandwiches! They all loved fried foods, including fish and chips, and ate a large number of burgers. Sweets, chocolates and biscuits were eaten daily. Their vegetable intake was limited – tomatoes, cucumber and, sometimes, broccoli.

Dairy foods are mucus forming, and consuming too many had impaired the older children's already delicate respiratory system. I felt the amount of saturated fat and sugar in their diet was contributing to their acne.

I asked Amanda to sprinkle Udo's Oil, which is rich in omega 3, 6 and 9, onto the children's cold food, or to give them a teaspoon of the oil daily. I also suggested she increase the children's intake of oily fish, to help increase the essential fatty acids in their diet. She also said she would try to give them a wider range of foods, to help balance their nutritional intake. Finally, I stressed that the children should drink more water to help eliminate toxins.

One month later, the children's skin was clearer and they suffered fewer asthma attacks.

'Water, like carbohydrates, proteins and fat, can be classed as a macronutrient as we need large quantities in our diet.'

Drink up: the importance of water

Water, like carbohydrates, proteins and fat, can be classed as a macronutrient as we need large quantities in our diet. Children especially need to top up their fluid levels frequently, as they are generally more active and have a faster metabolism than adults.

Micronutrients

Vitamins and minerals

We give our children oranges because they're full of vitamin C and encourage them to eat meat because it's rich in iron, but there is so much more we can teach them about vitamins and minerals, and that knowledge will transform the way they think about food. Vitamins and minerals are the workers behind the scene in a balanced diet, helping to keep the body in tune. They are also natural 'medicines' that can be given when there is a special need – for example, to ward off colds at the start of winter, or to reduce allergy symptoms in the summer.

Vitamins and minerals are found in almost all fresh foods. There are about 20 known vitamins, these work with one another and also with other nutrients. They can be either fat soluble or water soluble. They are essential in thousands of body processes, such as converting glucose into energy, and keeping everything from our skin and eyes, to lungs, bones and muscles, all functioning efficiently. They detoxify the body of harmful chemicals and keep our immune system in top condition. Deficiencies of these vital nutrients can cause a number of health problems, but excess can be equally harmful – how much you need of each depends on age, sex, health and lifestyle. It's essential to ensure your child's diet has a plentiful and balanced supply.

Does your child need supplements?

In an ideal world, your child would obtain all the vitamins they need from their diet. However, intensive farming methods have depleted the soil of nutrients, meaning that fewer end up in the food we harvest and consume. Processed food is also depleted of goodness. It may be that a vitamin and mineral supplement could be beneficial to your child's health, especially if they don't yet eat a wide range of foods. It is advisable to consult a nutritionist or paediatrician for advice on what supplements may be needed, and which are the most easily absorbed by the body.

Fat-soluble vitamins	
Vitamin A	This vitamin is connected with beauty as well as wellbeing. It is particularly good for night vision, skin health and to boost the immune system. Find it in veal, milk, egg yolk, spinach, broccoli and all orange and yellow fruits and vegetables.
Vitamin D	Obtained by exposure to sunlight and also found in some foods, including fish oils, egg yolk, fortified butter, margarine and cheeses. It is needed by the body to help absorption of calcium for healthy bones and teeth.
Vitamin E	A powerful antioxidant to protect all cell membranes. Dietary sources include vegetable oils, leafy greens and nuts. There are also smaller amounts in eggs and poultry.
Vitamin K	Helps the blood-clotting mechanism and the formation of other tissues. It is largely found in dark green vegetables, egg yolk and fish oils.

Water-soluble vitamins	
Vitamin B	The B vitamins are found in protein, including meat, fish, eggs, nuts, seeds, beans and wholegrains. They are important for the nervous system and are needed in the process of releasing energy from carbohydrates, proteins and fats.
Vitamin C	Found in fruit and vegetables, this important vitamin helps to boost immunity.

Minerals	
Calcium	Essential for strong bones and teeth. Calcium is found in dairy products, root vegetables, seeds and some nuts. These should be eaten with magnesium-rich foods (see below) to maximise its absorption. Foods that interfere with absorption of calcium include spinach, sugary foods and rhubarb. Try not to give these foods in excess to your child.
Magnesium	Magnesium functions alongside calcium, and is a very important mineral for muscles and nerves. It also works with B vitamins to help release energy from carbohydrates, proteins and fats. Good sources include leafy green vegetables, wholegrain cereals, nuts, seeds, beans and soya milk.
Potassium	Found in many fruits and vegetables, especially bananas. Deficiency can be found in the young, so it is important to make sure your child eats plenty of fresh produce. It helps to maintain the body's acid-alkaline balance.
Sodium	This mineral comes mainly from the salt in foods. Essential for nerve and muscle functioning and to regulate the body's fluid balance. An excess of sodium causes imbalances of other minerals and promotes high blood pressure and heart problems.
Iron	Iron is a trace element found in red meat, oatmeal, dried peaches, raisins, prunes, egg yolk, dried beans and leafy vegetables. It is essential for the formation of red blood cells.
Zinc	This trace element is needed for hormone production, mental function and immune resistance. Best sources include seafood, red meat, nuts, seeds, pulses and wholegrains.

Foods to cut back on

Now you know the essential elements of a good diet and what foods will provide them for your child. But there are also some foods that should be eaten only in moderation. The good thing is that by adding more nutrient-rich choices to your family's meals, there will automatically be less space on the table (and in your child's tummy) for poorer options.

- White bread – bread and white flour products are stripped of nutrients, and even 'enriched' versions won't contain all the goodness of wholegrain versions.

- High-fibre cereal – while some fibre is essential in the diet for efficient digestion, too much can cause a deficiency of important minerals including calcium, iron, and zinc.

- Sweets and chocolate – no parent should deny their child the occasional treat, but sweets and chocolate are high in sugar. This refined carbohydrate has no nutrients and can be bad for your child's teeth, can upset their intestinal flora and may suppress their immune system. Chocolate may contain hydrogenated fat (see cakes and biscuits, below). A chocolate bar that contains 70% cocoa solids will contain less sugar and fat than other varieties.

- Cakes and biscuits – partially hydrogenated fats (also known as trans fats) are found mainly in bought biscuits and cakes. They have been found to raise cholesterol and increase risk of heart disease.

- Salt (also called sodium on food labels) – commonly found in crisps, sausages, ham, bacon, snacks, ready meals and takeaways (75% of the salt we eat comes from processed foods). Excess salt may put stress on the kidneys and adrenal glands (responsible for releasing hormones like adrenaline), and is linked to high blood pressure.

- Fizzy drinks – these can be high in artificial flavourings, preservatives and colouring. The carbon dioxide and phosphoric acid used to make them fizz can inhibit the absorption of calcium.

- Processed meat – children may love foods such as burgers, sausages,

'Brown bread looks like wholewheat but the colour comes from additives. It's no better than white loaves.'

bacon and luncheon meat, but these are often high in nitrates (used as a preservative and linked to an increased risk of colon cancer), salt and saturated fat, and low in nutrients.

Quick tip

Read food labels! There is often hidden sugar in foods such as yoghurt, cereals, cakes, biscuits, canned foods, processed foods and salad dressing. Look for the words fructose, lactose, maltose, glucose, sucrose, syrup and molasses.

Recommended daily salt intakes

The Food Standards Agency has set salt targets for children:

- 7-12 months: 1g per day.
- 1-3 years: 2g per day.
- 4-6 years: 3g per day.
- 7-10 years: 5g per day.
- 11 years and above: 6g per day.

(Source: www.food.gov.uk, accessed 1 May 2010.)

Food additives

It's a myth that all food additives are harmful. Some of them are necessary as preservatives, to aid in the preparation of a food, or to help maintain its nutritional value. However, others may be artificial flavourings and colours that are used to make a product seem more attractive, disguising poor quality ingredients and inferior flavour.

Some additives, although legal for use in foods here in the UK, are the cause of health concerns. For example, salt and sugar are commonly used as preservatives, although it is accepted that eating too much of either of these may increase the risk of certain diseases.

Other additives may trigger a reaction in children and adults according to the Food Standards Agency. This can include an asthma attack, eczema, urticaria (nettle rash), dermatitis, or rhinitis (runny nose). If you believe your child may be reacting to an additive, read food labels carefully and consult your GP.

(Source: www.eatwell.gov.uk, accessed 1 May 2010.)

Some additives have also been linked to hyperactivity in children.

Common additives to cause reactions are:

Tartrazine (E102) – yellow colouring used in soft drinks, sweets, cakes and sauces. May cause urticaria, dermatitis, asthma, rhinitis and hyperactivity.

Sulphites, including sulphur dioxide – used as a preservative in soft drinks, processed meat and dried fruit and vegetables. May cause asthma attacks.

Benzoates – used in soft drinks and mackerel but found naturally in fruit and honey. They can worsen symptoms of asthma and eczema in children. Although its use is permitted, the Hyperactive Children's Support Group has put propyl 4-hydroxybenzonate (E216) on its exclusion list.

'Foods containing the following additives must be labelled "may have an adverse effect on activity and attention in children" – Tartrazine (E102), Quinoline Yellow (E104), Sunset Yellow (E110), Carmosine (E122), Ponceau 4R (E124), Allura Red (E129) and Sodium Benzoate.'

Summing Up

- Nutrients can be divided into carbohydrates, proteins, fats and water (macronutritents), and vitamins and minerals (micronutrients).

- Simple carbohydrates release energy quickly. While complex carbohydrates are higher in nutrients and will help your child to feel fuller for longer.

- Protein is essential for the growth and repair of the body's cells. It is broken down in the body into amino acids.

- Animal proteins contain all the amino acids your child needs. Vegetable proteins are incomplete and must be combined in order to supply the full range of amino acids.

- Fat is essential for many body processes, but some fats are linked with health problems.

- Vitamins and minerals are micronutrients essential to keep the body healthy.

- Certain foods should be reduced in your child's diet to promote good health and development.

- Some food additives can trigger reactions such as asthma, eczema and hyperactivity in children.

Chapter Three

Age Birth to One

Feeding your child their first foods is one of the most enjoyable, frustrating, messy, wonderful things you can do together. It's the beginning of a lifelong relationship with what they eat and helps to establish how your family enjoys and shares mealtimes.

Every child approaches the challenge differently. For each one happy to be fed by spoon, there will be another that rejects all cutlery in favour of fingers. One may quickly develop a taste for vegetables, another may eat them only when sweetened with pear or apple.

We're not going to pretend that encouraging your child to eat is always easy. There may be days when your lovingly pulped purée is speedily spat out, or you seem to spend more time picking peas off the floor than you do watching them being swallowed. But preparing your own baby foods whenever possible, and later making meals that the whole family can enjoy – even the newest members – is well worth it. Not only are you guaranteeing that your child eats a good range of nutrients from ingredients you have chosen yourself, but you're developing their taste for a wide range of flavours, textures and smells – all of which will help your child to savour food as they grow up, and make them less picky about the choices put in front of them.

So, invest in a plastic mat for under the table and go for it. We promise, those jars of baby food in the shops won't look so appealing when you see how easy, fun and inexpensive it is to rustle up your own child and health-friendly dishes.

'Feeding your child their first foods is one of the most enjoyable, frustrating, messy, wonderful things you can do together.'

Milk: the first food

By the time you read this book, you're probably already thinking about moving your child on from an exclusive milk diet to one incorporating fruits, vegetables and, in time, dairy products, pulses, fats, meat and fish. But although it's worth starting from birth when we talk about establishing lifelong healthy eating, it's never too late to start.

Breast milk

The government and World Health Organisation (WHO) advocate breastfeeding over bottle-feeding with formula milk and recommend that you feed your child with milk alone (breast or formula) for their first six months, and that it remains an important part of their diet for the first year of life. After six months, solid foods can gradually be introduced alongside breast or formula milk. There are a number of reasons for this:

- According to research compiled by WHO and the National Health Service (NHS), breast milk contains all the nutrients a baby needs for healthy growth and development for the first six months of life.

- The combination of nutrients in breast milk naturally changes as your child grows.

- Breast milk contains protective factors that may help to reduce your child's risk of infections such as gastroenteritis, respiratory infection and ear infection. (Source: www.nutrition.org.uk, accessed 2 May 2010.)

- Even if breastfeeding isn't a long-term option for whatever reason, feeding your child this way for the first few days after birth, when a mother's body produces colostrum, a natural substance rich in antibodies, can boost your child's immunity and may help to prevent future illnesses.

Formula milk

If you are unable to breastfeed for medical reasons or choose not to do so, be assured that milk formulas are developed to be as close to human milk as possible and offer a range of nutrients to help your child grow and develop. You can consult a GP, nutritionist or dietitian about the best formula for your child.

Cow's milk

Ideally, cow's milk should be introduced to babies from the age of one. It shouldn't be given as the sole source of milk until then as it contains insufficient iron or vitamins C and D for their needs.

Don't start solids too early

With a new baby, every milestone is exciting – the first time your child sits up alone, claps their hands or begins to crawl. Giving your child that first spoonful of baby rice is just as thrilling, which is why it's tempting to start them on solids sooner than is necessary. But there are sound reasons for waiting. Milk will supply all of your baby's nutritional needs for the first six months and there's no evidence to suggest that giving your child other foods before that time has any health advantage.

'Milk will supply all of your baby's nutritional needs for the first six months and there's no evidence to suggest that giving your child other foods before that time has any health advantage.'

- Your child can usually sit up, take in and swallow puréed food from five months, but it's only at six months that they can actively spoon-feed – that is, use their lips to take the food from the spoon, chew it, and use their tongue to move it to the back of their mouth.

- At this age your child will have sufficient hand-eye co-ordination to pick up finger foods, and will be curious to try new tastes and textures.

- Your child's gut and kidneys will also have matured enough to cope with a broader diet – introduce solids before six months and there is an increased risk of infection and the development of allergies such as asthma and eczema, especially if there is a history of allergy in the family.

- There's no evidence that waiting until six months will affect your child's ability to chew or make them more likely to be a fussy eater.

But don't wait too long

Waiting longer than six months to wean your child isn't advised, as they need to replenish the stores of iron and other essential nutrients that they built up before birth. Delaying their introduction to the tastes and textures of food can also make eating solids more of a challenge, leading to unwanted stress at the dinner table for you and your child.

Signs your baby is ready for solids

Both the WHO and NHS recommend waiting until six months before starting your child on solid foods, but they also recognise that each child is individual and may not fit the averaged results from research conducted on thousands of babies. These are the signs that show your child is ready to expand their diet and move beyond the world of milk:

- They can sit up with support.

- They are taking an interest in what the rest of the family is eating.

- They are reaching out for your food.

- They are picking up and tasting finger foods.

- Their tongue-thrust reflex has gone. To test, mix up some baby rice and feed your child a tiny amount. If after several tries they still push it out of their mouth with their tongue, they aren't yet ready for spoon-feeding.

Six to seven months: weaning

So, the big day is here – what will your child's first solid food be? Baby rice is a good option as it is easily digested by most babies and its bland taste won't make too much of a change from their usual milk. Keep the consistency runny (food at this age is 'solid' in name only) by thinning with milk or boiled and cooled water, and make just a teaspoon or two at first.

Don't worry if your child seems to find it difficult to swallow this new food at first. They will be used to drinking milk and it may take a day or two to learn how to use their tongue to bring food to the back of their mouth.

After a few days, try introducing a single-variety fruit or vegetable purée. Babies have a sweet tooth, so apple or pear make a tempting spoonful. It may be wiser, though, to try a naturally sweet vegetable such as parsnip or carrot instead – you don't want your child to reject vegetables because they'd rather have fruit.

Although it's exciting to tick off all the new foods that your child will eat, it's important to introduce each item individually and to give it exclusively for two to three days, so that you can be sure it doesn't cause a reaction. Excessive wind, diarrhoea, being sick, a runny nose or watering eyes, a rash around the mouth or bottom, or waking in the night are all signs that your child may be sensitive to the food. If that happens, wait a couple of weeks and try them with it again. If they react in the same way, avoid the food until your child is at least a year old, when you can have another go.

How to prepare purées

▦ Babies need soft foods for those first mouthfuls, so start by steaming fruits and vegetables – this will reserve as many nutrients as possible. Alternatively, boil them in a little water in a saucepan.

▦ Use a food processor, blender, or mouli (see Baby's Kitchen Kit on page 41) to mash them into a smooth purée – add a little of the cooking water to thin, if necessary.

▦ As your child gains teeth and becomes better at eating, you will be able to introduce more texture into their meals. Vegetables can be mashed more roughly or lightly cooked and given as finger food, and fruit can be grated or puréed raw.

'Never leave your child alone while they eat because of the risk of choking.'

Storing and heating food

- Freshly cooked fruit or vegetables can be cooled and kept in the fridge for feeds during the day.

- To make your life simpler, cook more than you need and freeze the excess in ice cube trays. When they're solid, put the cubes in bags, label and store them in the freezer.

- Ice cubes will take about an hour to defrost, so just take out the cubes you need for the day's meals in the morning, pop them in bowls and keep them in the fridge until it's time for your baby to eat.

- Either take them out of the fridge half an hour or so before mealtime to let them reach room temperature, or pop the bowl in another bowl of hot water to warm gently.

Portion sizes

As your child becomes used to eating more than milk, their appetite will gradually increase and you can boost their portion sizes, going from a few spoonfuls, around 50g, of food at each meal, to 200g to 300g. Remember, at this age your child will still be having around three milk feeds (breast or formula) per day. Their body will tell them naturally when they have had enough to eat, so don't ask them to finish their bowlful if it's obvious they don't want it.

Quick tip

Don't give your child honey until they are one year old. It occasionally contains a bacteria called Clostridium botulinum that can make babies very ill.

Q&A – water and other drinks

It's not just new foods you introduce to your child, it's new drinks, too. Here's the lowdown on moving on from milk.

Q. Do babies need extra fluids?

A. Additional drinks for your child aren't really an issue until they reach six months of age. Until then, breastfed babies do not require any extra fluids, including water, as breast milk will naturally meet all their food and hydration needs. Formula-fed babies can be given a little boiled and cooled water. At six months, you will begin to decrease the amount of milk you give to your child, but don't let their fluid intake drop overall. Make up the difference with water or diluted fruit juices (see below).

Q. Is it okay to give my baby tap water?

A. Yes, as long as you boil and cool it if your child is younger than six months old. Some bottled waters are high in minerals and aren't safe for babies to drink. And while some may be labelled as safe for babies, they are not sterile and again will need to be boiled and cooled if your child hasn't reached six months in age.

Q. Should I filter tap water?

A. Filtering tap water in hard water areas can improve its taste, making it more appealing for your child. Filters also remove any potentially harmful materials such as lead, chlorine and bacteria from water. However, filtered water will still need to be boiled.

Q. Should I use a bottle or a cup?

A. Your child will need to learn how to sip from a cup and give up the bottle at some point, so it's a good idea to introduce the idea of using a cup as they move on from exclusively drinking milk. While cups with spouts are great when you're out and about, they won't teach your child to drink properly. For that, start by putting just a mouthful of water into the bottom of a one or two-handled cup, hold it to their lips and pour a few drops into their mouth. Let your child swallow then give them a bit more until they show they've had enough. With practise, they'll soon be able to take in more than they spill! If your child resists drinking this way, leave it for a couple of weeks then try again.

Q. Can my baby have juice?

A. Freshly made fruit and vegetable juices are a great way to introduce a baby to new flavours, and they're packed full of healthy vitamins, minerals, enzymes and other nutrients. But be sure to dilute them and be careful not to give your child too much – breast or formula milk should be their main drink for the first year. Too much juice can reduce their appetite for milk and cause diarrhoea, stomach cramps and tooth decay. Avoid acidic juices such as orange and grapefruit, which can cause stomach upsets. Examples of non-acidic juices are carrot juice, apple juice, pear juice and mango juice.

Q. What about other drinks?

A. Milk, water and a little bit of juice really are the best drinks for your child. Other options, such as diluted squash and fizzy pop, don't have any nutritional value and may contain harmful additives such as sweeteners, colourings and flavourings.

'Once your child is used to eating, you can begin to add more flavour, texture and nutrients to their diet.'

Seven to nine months – introducing protein

Once your child is used to eating, you can begin to add more flavour, texture and nutrients to their diet. Fish, particularly oily varieties (not shellfish), poultry and easily digested pulses, such as lentils, are rich in protein and iron. Iron is important for your child around this age, as babies are born with a store that lasts for around six months so it will be almost empty. The food you give them now should help to replenish your child's supplies, especially as iron deficiency is not easy to spot.

You will still need to purée these foods at first, increasing the chunkiness as your child gets better at chewing and swallowing. Mix them with vegetables and carbohydrates, such as wholemeal bread and pasta, for a mini but balanced meal.

Doing it for themselves

Around this age, those sticky fingers are likely to reach out for the spoon you are feeding with, or grab and prod the food in their bowl. It might be messy, but don't discourage this self feeding – it's a vital developmental step, and essential if your child is to learn to feed themselves properly.

- Give your child an identical spoon to the one you are feeding them with, so mealtimes don't become a fight over cutlery.

- Let your child play with their food, within reason. Exploring the feel of food is the first step to a love of food and healthy eating.

- Provide a range of soft finger foods to keep your child interested at the table. Slices of peeled fruit, such as apple and banana, steamed vegetables such as carrot sticks and broccoli, soft strips of chicken and pieces of wholemeal toast are good options.

Is my child too fat?

Most babies are quite chubby at this age. Don't worry – as they begin to crawl and walk, your child should begin to lose any excess weight.

Nine to 12 months – family meals

At this stage, you should be able to give your child at least some of the meals that you cook for the whole family, making mealtimes simpler, cheaper and a real shared experience – just remember to add any salt or sugar to your meal after you have spooned out your child's portion.

Your child's daily menu should now look like yours, with three main meals a day – breakfast, lunch and dinner – plus a few healthy snacks and plenty of water to drink. You should be able to retire your blender now, and instead chop, grate, or mash your child's food. Your child's appetite will be growing as they do, so you might want to give them two courses at lunch and dinner – fruit, fromage frais and yoghurt make great puddings.

> ## Quick tip
>
> Even if you're not eating a meal, try to have some food along with your child. It will encourage them to tuck in.

The building blocks of a healthy diet

Try to make sure your child has a wide range of foods to eat. This will provide them with the vitamins and minerals they need. It will also introduce them to lots of different flavours, making them less likely to be fussy eaters later on. Don't be scared to give your child stronger flavours such as garlic, herbs and spices.

- Give your child one to two servings of protein each day – try softly cooked fish, meat, beans and lentils.
- They will also need two to three servings of carbohydrate each day – bread, rice, pasta and potatoes are good, inexpensive sources.
- Give your child fruit and vegetables at every meal and as snacks.
- Make sure your child eats dairy foods such as cheese, fromage frais and yoghurt.
- They will also need breast milk or around 600ml formula per day.

> ## Quick tip
>
> If your child doesn't like a certain food, don't force them to eat it. Try giving it to them again in a few weeks, chances are they'll be ready to give it a go.

Vegetarian babies

A well-balanced, varied vegetarian diet can provide all the nutrients your child needs to develop and thrive. However, you will need to ensure that the nutrients usually provided by meat and fish are supplied from other sources. It is a good idea to consult your GP, a dietitian or nutritionist for advice on how to combine protein sources to ensure your child receives all the essential amino acids they need in their diet.

- Give your child two servings of vegetable protein per day with a carbohydrate such as rice – try pulses such as lentils, chickpeas and beans, and eggs and tofu.

- Serve fruit and vegetables along with non-meat protein, not just as snacks – the vitamin C in them will help your child to absorb more iron.

- Remember that the proteins in a vegetarian diet need to be well complemented, to provide good health and energy – see page 19.

Vegan diets

A vegan diet restricts foods that are animal in origin. As a result, it can be difficult to ensure your child receives all the nutrients they need, especially complete proteins, iron, calcium, and vitamins B and D. If you are planning to wean your child on to a vegan diet, it is essential to consult a GP, dietitian or nutritionist first.

Baby's kitchen kit

You don't need a lot of expensive kitchen equipment to cook for your child. Here are the basics:

- Small, stainless steel saucepan.

- Steamer.

- Hand-held blender, mouli or food processor.

- Ice cube trays.

- Freezer bags.

- Small bowls.

- Soft spoons.

- Highchair.
- Plastic mat to go under highchair.
- Bibs.
- Beaker or cup.

Cooking safely

You probably cook with food safety in mind anyway, but here are a few tips to help you avoid food poisoning for you and your child:

- Keep raw and cooked meats separate to avoid contamination.
- Wash your hands with soap and water before preparing food, and again if you touch raw meat, fish or eggs. Make sure your hands are clean before feeding your child.
- Refrigerate or freeze cooked food as soon as it is cool.
- Only serve as much food as you think your child will eat, then top up if necessary. Don't save any leftovers for a later meal – saliva transferred from your child's mouth to the food by the spoon will begin to digest the food and it may start to go off.

Great first foods – six months	Foods to avoid
<ul><li>Baby rice.</li><li>Porridge.</li><li>Low-salt and sugar breakfast cereals (Ready Brek, Shreddies).</li><li>Fruit (but not citrus fruits or berries).</li><li>Vegetables.</li><li>Chicken.</li><li>Turkey.</li></ul>	<ul><li>Added sugar and salt.</li><li>Butter and oil.</li><li>Red meat.</li><li>Honey (until one year).</li><li>Nuts (until one year; five if there is a family history of allergy).</li><li>Citrus fruits and berries.</li><li>Shellfish (until five years).</li><li>Be careful with wheat and gluten for the first year.</li><li>Seeds.</li><li>Semi skimmed milk.</li></ul>

Great first foods – six to nine months	Foods to avoid
▪ White fish. ▪ Finger foods – pasta, raw and cooked vegetables, fruit.	▪ Added sugar and salt. ▪ Honey (until one year). ▪ Nuts (until one year; five if there is a family history of allergy). ▪ Shellfish (until five years). ▪ Seeds. ▪ Wheat and Gluten.

Great first foods – nine to 12 months	Foods to avoid
▪ Citrus fruits and berries. ▪ Yoghurt. ▪ Cheese. ▪ Pulses. ▪ Oily fish. ▪ Red meat.	▪ Added sugar and salt. ▪ Honey (until one year). ▪ Nuts (until one year; five if there is a family history of allergy). ▪ Shellfish (until five years).

Summing Up

- Babies should be given breast milk or formula exclusively until they are six months old.

- Weaning on to baby rice and puréed fruits and vegetables can begin at six months old.

- At seven to nine months you can introduce protein and make the texture of purées chunkier.

- From nine months, your child can eat the same dishes as the rest of the family (with no added salt or sugar) and have three meals, plus snacks, per day.

- A balanced diet for your child will include protein, carbohydrates, fruit, vegetables and dairy foods.

- Some children are at higher risk of food allergies.

- Care needs to be taken with vegetarian and vegan diets to ensure your child receives sufficient nutrients.

Chapter Four

Ages One to Five

It's hard to imagine when you're watching your child play with their peas or refusing to eat anything but a bowl of cereal, but the memory of childhood meals will inform your child's food choices as an adult, even as they develop their own tastes and seek out different recipes and new flavours to try. Get the basics right and your child can build a healthy lifestyle around what you have taught them simply by serving up quick, tasty and healthy dinners.

You don't have to be an amateur chef or spend a fortune on ingredients to serve up delicious family meals. And although it's not always easy for working parents or carers to fit in a job, grocery shopping, childcare and all the other demands on your time, it should be possible to serve up home-cooked food at least part of the week. You could sit down as a family and decide together when it's most important to you to share a meal, whether that's breakfast, lunch or dinner – even once a week is better than nothing.

Of course, making good food choices is more likely to happen when eating is associated with fun, rather than stress or pressure. Which is why in this chapter you'll find ideas for encouraging your child to eat a great range of healthy meals, without using food as either punishment or reward. There's also common sense advice about balancing treats, a word on the pitfalls of sugar and immunity-boosting superfoods for children aged up to five.

'You don't have to be an amateur chef or spend a fortune on ingredients to serve up delicious family meals.'

Superfoods for kids

Small children are a blank canvas when it comes to bugs, which is why they tend to come down with so many colds, stomach upsets and other viruses. Your kitchen can act as a natural medicine cabinet to keep your child as healthy as possible and aid their recovery when they do feel poorly. Eating a wide range of fresh, natural foods will provide a broad spectrum of essential nutrients that will help to make your child more resistant to illness. Use the list below and fill your cupboards with foods that are packed with vitamins to boost the body's natural immunity, antioxidants to fight cell damage, and slow-releasing energy to help keep your child going, whether they're feeling on top of the world or under the weather.

Fruit

Apples

Apples are popular with children and provide a range of good nutrients including vitamin C, fibre and powerful antioxidants that boost the immune system. They are rich in pectin, which stimulates the bacteria in the gut, and they contain fibre, which helps to prevent constipation in children. Wash them well and, if possible, do not peel them before serving to your child.

Apricots

Children love the sweet taste of fresh or dried apricots. They are rich in vitamin C to protect the body from colds and recurrent infections. They are also rich sources of phytochemicals, which are good for skin health. If you buy dried apricots, or any other dried fruits, make sure you choose those preserved without sulphur dioxide (it will be marked on the label), as this can cause allergic reactions in some children.

Grapes

Grapes and raisins are sweet snacks that make a great alternative to chocolate and confectionery. Both are rich in vitamins and fibre. Raisins (like all dried fruit) are high in sugar, so only a small handful should be given as a treat or when your child needs a burst of energy.

Berries

Wonder foods for kids – blueberries, blackberries, cherries, raspberries, strawberries and blackcurrants are all rich in bioflavonoids (minerals such as zinc, iron and isoflavones), antioxidants, vitamin C, potassium and calcium. Keep berries in the fridge to maintain their nutrient content.

Bananas

Rich in potassium, vitamins C and B6, beta carotene and fibre – and kids love them. The tryptophan is relaxing and helps to aid sleep, although bananas are also great when a quick burst of energy is needed. Choose ripe bananas for children, as they are more easily digested.

Citrus fruits

These are renowned for their high vitamin C content, which helps to strengthen children's immune systems against viruses, colds and infections. However, citrus fruits such as lemons, oranges and grapefruit are also packed with fibre, folic acid, pectin, phytochemicals and flavonoids, all of which supercharge wellbeing.

Kiwi fruit

Children love them cut in half and served in an egg cup with a spoon to scoop out the flesh. Kiwi fruits are packed with vitamin C, potassium and fibre.

Nuts and seeds

Nuts, nut butters and seeds make a great energy-boosting food and they are packed with nutrients to help boost your child's immunity. Serve nuts either chopped or ground to avoid any risk of choking, until your little one is five.

Walnuts

These are rich in protein, vitamins B6 and E, potassium, magnesium and omega 3. They're great for boosting immunity.

Almonds

This nutritious nut is high in essential fatty acids, which are good for the heart, and magnesium, which helps children to relax.

'Always wash fresh and dried fruit well to remove any traces of dirt and pesticides.'

Nuts and allergy

Nuts should be avoided below the age of five if there is any family history of allergies. Even if there is no known risk, watch carefully for signs of a reaction the first time your child has nuts; this is likely to come on within minutes of eating them and no more than four hours afterwards.

Signs of a mild allergic reaction to nuts include:

- Tingling lips and mouth.
- Swelling of the face.
- Feeling sick.
- A rash, similar to nettle rash.
- Stomach pains.
- Tightening of the throat.

More serious symptoms include:

- Difficulty breathing.
- Fast heart rate.
- Faintness or dizziness.

Sesame seeds

Rich in calcium, these make a good addition to the diet if your child is sensitive to dairy products. They are also high in antioxidant vitamin E and many other nutrients.

Sunflower seeds

These seeds are wonderful ground over muesli, breakfast cereal or yoghurt to supercharge your child's breakfast. They are a good source of essential fatty acids, boosting brain function.

Pumpkin seeds

These have some of the highest zinc levels of all the seeds, so should be given from an early age to help support the immune system. They are also a good source of protein, magnesium, potassium and omega 6 and omega 9 essential fatty acids.

Linseeds (flaxseeds)

These are very rich in omega 3 essential fatty acids. Grind them over breakfast cereals or put a few drops of flaxseed oil into smoothies or salad dressings but do not use for cooking.

Vegetables

Broccoli, cabbage, cauliflower and Brussels sprouts

These vegetables, called brassicas, are rich in fibre and contain important nutrients including iron, folic acid, beta carotene and vitamin K. They do have a strong taste, which some children find off putting, but try mixing in small amounts with other vegetables until your child is used to the flavour.

Carrots

Sweet and colourful, this popular vegetable has high levels of beta carotene, which is converted to vitamin A in the body and helps to protect against viruses and infections. Carrots are a great food to boost immunity and liver function. Complexion-friendly beta carotene is wonderful for children with skin conditions such as eczema.

Tomatoes

Most kids love tomatoes and they're perfect for snacking on between meals or served in a mini salad with dinner. As well as immunity-boosting vitamin C, they contain lycopene, a powerful antioxidant that helps to prevent cell damage. Try to cut back on the ketchup, if you can!

Garlic, onion and leeks

This family of vegetables has antiseptic, antiviral and antibacterial properties. Garlic also acts as a potent antibiotic. It contains allicin, which is released only when the garlic is chopped or crushed, and seems to have potential health benefits. They are also high in vitamin C and the mineral selenium, which plays an important role in protecting against cancer and heavy metal toxicity.

Mushrooms

A good source of nutrients, including B vitamins, protein, iron, folic acid and zinc. Zinc is important, as a lack is linked to poor resistance to infections, skin conditions such as eczema and sleeplessness in young children.

Sweet potatoes

Children love the sweet taste of this vegetable. It makes a great addition to vegetable soups and can also be baked or mashed. Sweet potatoes are packed with vitamin C, calcium, magnesium and beta carotene. Calcium and magnesium work together on the body's chemistry, helping to maintain a healthy nervous system. Sweet potato even promotes strong teeth and healthy gums in children.

Green beans

These vegetables are a favourite of children. They are rich in vitamins A and C, and are a good food for helping skin disorders.

Four ways with vegetables

One of the wonderful aspects of vegetables is that they can be prepared in so many different ways, which gives you the chance to find the method that suits your child best. Remember to wash vegetables well before cooking and eating, peeling and removing seeds where necessary to minimise the risk of choking. Try these ways of serving up your veg:

- Raw – fingers of sweet pepper and cucumber, grated carrot, whole mange tout and mini corn, tiny cherry tomatoes, or wands of celery. Kids love to pick up and play with their food, and there's no better way than by dipping raw veg into hummus, eating celery filled with soft cheese, or simply seeing how many different colour crudités they can fill their plate with. The amazing thing about raw vegetables is that their natural enzymes aren't killed off by cooking, meaning the body can access them for a huge range of functions, including aiding digestion and providing energy.

- Steamed – lightly steaming vegetables makes them easy and tasty to eat, while preserving as many of their nutrients as possible (these can leach into the cooking water if you boil them). If your child prefers, drizzle steamed vegetables with extra virgin olive oil and lemon.

- Roasted – this method of cooking is fantastic for sweet or starchy vegetables – the heat of the oven intensifies their flavour and deepens their colour for a beautiful looking plateful. If your child doesn't enjoy them at first, try changing the oil you roast them in – olive oil and hemp oil are good options.

- Soups and juices – while you wait for your child to fall in love with broccoli, you can try these tricks to increase their vegetable intake: make a vegetable soup (great served with a crouton of bread and toasted cheese); purée the vegetables and use them as a sauce with rice or a small type of pasta; disguise loathed vegetables with those your child does like, such as stirring puréed peppers or carrots into a favourite tomato sauce; and make delicious juices that introduce them to the taste of vegetables before they try them again whole (you can dilute vegetable juices with water or combine with fruit juices to make them more palatable).

Pulses and beans

Children often love pulses and beans, and may actually find them easier to chew and digest than meat. They are a great choice – as well as protein, legumes contain both soluble and insoluble fibres to keep the intestinal tract healthy, and they provide a good source of vitamins, minerals such as zinc and iron and isoflavones. Beans are a great store cupboard food, as the dried varieties can keep for up to a year if stored in a dry, cool place in an airtight container. See chapter 2 on what foods to eat with pulses and beans to ensure your child gets the right protein balance.

Lentils

Lentils are a good source of vegetable protein, some B vitamins and a significant amount of iron, calcium, magnesium, zinc and folic acid. Eating foods rich in vitamin C with lentils will increase the absorption of iron. Young children often prefer the mild orange lentils, but green and brown lentils are excellent cooked in stews and casseroles.

'Children often love pulses and beans, and may actually find them easier to chew and digest than meat.'

Chickpeas

Wonderful in stews and salads, or puréed into home-made hummus. Chickpeas are rich in calcium, magnesium, zinc, potassium, beta carotene and folic acid.

Peas

Children love this bright, sweet vegetable and it loves them – peas strengthen digestion and improve constipation. High in thiamin (vitamin B1), vitamin C and niacin.

Soya

Soya is packed with protein, fibre, thiamine, iron and added calcium.

Eating by colours

By serving meals that combine as many colours as possible, we maximise the range of nutrients our child has in one sitting, because different colours are associated with certain health benefits.

Eating by colours is a great way of helping you to plan menus. Picturing the colours of breakfast, lunch or dinner is a quick way of checking that the meal has a good balance of vitamins, minerals, proteins, carbohydrates and fats. It also fires your child's imagination about what they are eating.

White	Fish, chicken, turkey and dairy products.
Brown	Grains, pulses and nuts.
Orange	Carrots, apricots, swede, mango and papaya.
Yellow	Egg yolk, sweet corn, lemon and pineapple.
Green	Fruit and vegetables.
Pink	Salmon and seafood.
Blue	Berries.
Red	Peppers, berries, tomatoes and plums.

How much fish?

The government recommends that everybody should eat at least two 140g portions of fish per week, one of which should be oily. However, due to pollutants that are absorbed by fish as they feed, it's important to follow guidelines for your child. (Source: 'How much oily fish?' Food Standards Agency, www.eatwell.gov.uk, accessed 29 June 2010.)

- Girls under the age of 16 should eat no more than two portions per week of oily fish, although they can eat unlimited white fish.
- Boys under the age of 16 can have up to four portions of oily fish and unlimited white fish.
- Girls and boys under the age of 16 should avoid marlin, shark and swordfish.
- Tinned tuna counts as white fish, as the oils are lost in the canning process.
- Shellfish, such as crabs, prawns and shrimps, can cause allergic reactions, so it is best to avoid giving them to children younger than five.

Sugar – the treat that's not so sweet

Most children are born with a sweet tooth, which is wonderful – the natural sugars in carrots and parsnips, squash and sweet peppers, melons and mangoes are all great ways to tempt your child into eating healthy, delicious foods. But of course, that isn't the only sugar they're exposed to. Cakes, biscuits, chocolate and sweets are all full of sugar, which if eaten in excess can lead to health and behaviour problems for your child. And it isn't just sweet treats that are a problem. Refined foods that are low in fibre and high in simple carbohydrates are converted rapidly into glucose in the body, pushing blood sugar high above normal levels.

It's best to limit the number of sweet foods your child eats from an early age. Rewarding, comforting or quietening your child with sweets sets up a connection between 'being good' or 'feeling better' and sugar, which can lead to unhealthy eating habits in later life. Excess sugar can also lead to the following problems:

- Mood changes – too much sugar can make your child feel irritable, moody, depressed, hyperactive or tired. One of the reasons for this is that refined foods are depleted of B vitamins. B-vitamin deficiency (especially B1) can cause or aggravate depression, anxiety and other behavioural changes.

- Cravings – the way that the body processes excess sugar can actually lead to a desire for more, ultimately putting your child's organs under strain as they try to cope with sharp highs and lows in blood sugar levels.

- Tooth decay – sugar can increase bacteria in the mouth, creating an acid environment. The acid attacks the enamel of teeth, making them more prone to decay.

- Long-term health problems – when sugar and refined foods are eaten in excess, the sugar contained in them disturbs the metabolism of glucose in the body, contributing to diabetes, hypoglycaemia (low blood sugar), high blood pressure and heart problems. The rise in child diabetes has been linked with high sugar intake.

- Obesity – although there is a genetic link to obesity, it can be dealt with satisfactorily with good nutrition, part of which is monitoring sugar levels.

- Weakened immune system – too much sugar has been associated with a reduction in the amount of minerals available to the body to help fight disease.

- Intestinal disorders – excess sugar disturbs the balance of the gut.

The sugar cycle explained

The human body is designed to convert the carbohydrate in food into a sugar called glucose, which gives your child the energy to run around in the playground, climb trees or simply annoy their siblings! Blood glucose is controlled by two hormones released by the pancreas (insulin and glucagon), which increase and decrease glucose levels according to the body's needs. When we eat a meal containing simple carbohydrates (refined products or sugar), the food is digested and absorbed quickly, pushing our blood sugar level well above its normal level. This triggers the pancreas into releasing insulin, which diffuses the glucose. This quick removal of blood glucose causes a drop in energy in the body and we crave more sugary foods. A negative cycle has begun.

The ultimate sugar fix

The key to balancing the sugar level in your child's body is to slow down the production of glucose. If you prevent a spike in their blood sugar and the subsequent release of insulin, you'll stop the sudden dramatic fall in glucose that leads to a dip in energy and the craving for more sugar. The aim is to eat foods that provide a steady release of energy. Here's how:

- Give your child complex carbohydrates, such as wholemeal pasta and bread, rather than refined versions that release sugar more quickly into the body.

- Combine simple carbohydrates with fibre, which will help to slow down digestion and the release of sugar.

- Pair carbohydrates with protein, which will again help to release glucose more slowly.

- Read labels carefully – juices that claim 'no added sugar' may be rich in fructose, the natural fruit sugar, which has the same effect on dental decay as sugar. If you can, make your own fruit juices and dilute them with water. Otherwise, add water to bought fresh juices.

- Choose sweet treats wisely – rather than sugary cereals, pick varieties that are sweetened with raisins and other dried fruit – although high in sugar, they are also rich in fibre and nutrients.

- Get baking – making your own pastries, cakes and biscuits is fun for you and your child. Adapt recipes so that you use wholemeal flour (try swapping white flour for wholemeal, or use a mix of 50:50 white flour and wholemeal) and reduced sugar – they'll still taste delicious.

Finding your family's healthy balance

When it comes to food, every family needs to find a balance of health and convenience that works for them. It will depend on the number of children you have, the time you have to shop and cook in, the types of food you like to eat and what you can afford to spend. Don't let providing good meals turn into another pressure in an already full life. If you aim to provide a healthy diet for 80% of the time, you can go with the flow for the remaining 20% (as long as your child has no particular health problems).

A nutritious breakfast is always a good start. Fruit, nuts, seeds and vegetables make healthy snacks for mid-morning or afternoon. Lunch should provide a mix of protein, vegetables and healthy fats. Dinner should be early to give your child time to digest their meal before bed, and feature seasonal fruits and vegetables – home-made soup, pasta or rice with a little protein, served with vegetables. And the occasional biscuit or cake can add a touch of sweetness to the day.

Summing Up

- The meals you serve your child now will influence their food choices as an adult.

- Eating a broad range of natural foods will help to boost your child's immunity to illness and help them to recover more quickly.

- Be aware of signs of nut allergy.

- Meals that contain foods of lots of different colours will contain a broad range of nutrients.

- Too much sugar can have a negative impact on your child's health and behaviour.

- Every family should find its own healthy food balance.

Chapter Five

Ages Six to 10

When children cook, they become part of a magic show – turning basic foodstuffs into meals. It's a spellbinding lesson and it allows young ones to discover the wonder of ingredients. This is the perfect age to start your child's exploration of the kitchen (supervised by you, of course). And while they are finding out how to chop, stir and season, you can also teach them how each food works in the body, helping them to grow up healthy and strong.

This chapter will look at how to encourage your child to eat a wide range of foods, because even a child who loves to cook may need a little extra encouragement to swallow their greens sometimes. It will also tackle the tricky subject of the school lunch box and provide ideas for healthy meals and snacks for six to 10 year olds.

After the play-focused learning of the reception class, these are the years when school becomes more demanding. The information here on essential vitamins and brain-boosting foods will help you to give your child a nutritional foundation for effective learning and power them through sports days, plays and after-school activities.

'Cooking with children is messy, but it's worth it to watch how much they enjoy eating food they have prepared themselves.'

Starting to cook

It's never too early to begin teaching your child about how food is prepared. Babies can be brought into the kitchen in their highchairs so that they can watch you make dinner while keeping out of harm's way. A toddler can help to stir a cake mixture, a three or four year old can help to roll out pastry, and a child of five or six can begin to measure out ingredients and even chop up vegetables, under your watchful eye. Outside of the kitchen, they can play with toy foodstuffs, pretending to cook or buy groceries. On your own weekly shop, your child can help to choose fresh fruits and vegetables and talk about what meals you will make with them.

Children love to slice up cucumber, celery and tomatoes to make a side salad (younger children can use a plastic knife). They can't wait to knead the dough for home-made pizza or sieve flour for biscuits. Yes, they make a mess, but it's worth it to see how much they enjoy eating what they have prepared – a great tip for any parent who wants their child to eat more vegetables. This 'game' also teaches them the importance of food hygiene, as you teach them to wash their hands before they start and at the end of cooking, and make sure surfaces and equipment are clean.

Quick tip

When cooking with your child, it's best to use only a few utensils at a time and explain why you've chosen each one – a large saucepan for boiling pasta, say, or a washable chopping board for preparing meat. Keep knives and other sharp objects far from reach and make sure they don't go near the oven or hob.

Tips for fussy eaters

Nothing ruins a child's appetite like tension at the dinner table, and that's especially true when your little one is reluctant to eat a certain food. As parents, it can be hard to stay calm and detached as your child pushes their peas around their plate or won't swallow their roast chicken. The strategies below may help, but remember, you know your child best and it's you who will understand whether gentle encouragement, fun and joking, a reward chart or another approach will suit them best when it comes to tackling what's on their plate.

- Discuss together, before you go to the shops, what your child wants to eat and what you would like them to try. Plan menus and meals as a team.

- Involve your child in preparing and cooking meals when you can.

- Talk about where different foods come from and why they are good for you.

60

- Use fun images to get your child excited about eating. Why not say that all the healthy foods are invited to a party in their tummy – couldn't they eat their carrots so they could join the broccoli for some fun?

- Explain that there are no bad foods, but that some need to be eaten in smaller amounts to help keep them feeling strong and healthy.

- Have fun with the way you present food. Try making faces on the plate with it and that smiling food friend will soon be in your child's stomach.

- Invite your child's friends around for tea, so they can enjoy eating together – children will often try previously refused foods when they see their friends enjoying them.

- Keep a healthy stock of fruit, vegetables, wholegrains, lean proteins and healthy cheeses in the kitchen and explain why you have chosen them. Simply seeing foods frequently can help them to become familiar and inspire your child to try them out.

There are some cases where you need to let your child lead. For example, you will come to know when they genuinely don't like a certain food or a particular way of preparing it – for example, some children will happily eat mince but find it difficult to swallow roast beef. As long as they are eating a wide range of other foods, an occasional 'no' shouldn't leave a nutritional gap in their diet. Never push your child to eat a food that they have had a bad experience with, such as choking or burning their tongue because a mouthful was too hot. In this case, let them try it again in their own time.

Case study: a picky eater

Seven-year-old Robert was brought to see me because he suffered from frequent colds and tummy aches. Talking with his mother, Rosa, it became clear that Robert's diet was high in sugary food and fatty snacks, and overloaded with dairy products and milk. Robert was apparently very picky about what foods he would eat, and Rosa said she had tried everything possible to make him eat a larger variety, with no success.

Robert's repetitive diet was lacking in the nutrients found in good fats, vegetables and fruit. As a result, his immune system had become weakened. Dairy products can increase the formation of excessive mucus, and the large quantity he ate was not helping his frequent colds. Rather than cutting out dairy foods altogether, I gave him a list of a few products he could eat, so as not to frighten him with a drastic change to his diet. The continual intake of sugary foods impoverished the friendly bacteria in his gut, causing tummy problems. Refined carbohydrates (white flour products) are not as nutritious as complex carbohydrates such as wholegrains. They also caused his blood sugar level to drop too fast, causing him to crave more sugary foods.

I explained to Robert that our body is like a car, with the brain as its motor. The body is a very complex piece of machinery and needs to be fuelled with good petrol. Carbohydrates such as bread, pasta and rice are the petrol; protein, including meat, fish and pulses, are the building blocks that renew and repair the machinery; and fats such as olive oil and fish oils keep the machine lubricated and functioning smoothly. Vitamins and minerals in fruit and vegetables are the hidden helpers that make sure that every part of the machine (body) works well with the others.

Robert told me that he wanted to be an astronaut when he grew up, and I encouraged him to eat more healthily to feed his brain and body, so that he would be fit and strong enough to go for his goal.

Three months later, Rosa told me that Robert was a completely different boy; he always ate vegetables with his meals, snacked on fruit instead of sweet treats, and no longer suffered from poor health. It really does help to explain to a child the way that foods work in the body and that eating a balanced diet will bring them closer to achieving their dreams.

'Explaining that the body is like a motor and that it needs fuel and the right parts to make it run, will encourage your child to eat.'

Case study: the boy who didn't like vegetables

The only vegetables that Ann's little boy Mark, aged six, would eat were peas, potatoes and carrots – those that taste the sweetest.

I explained to Ann that most young children prefer sweet-tasting vegetables but that they develop a liking for stronger flavours as they mature. Sometimes, however, a little one like Mark can become 'stuck' in his food choices and refuse to try anything new.

I told Ann that the next time Mark refused to eat a vegetable, she should remove it from the table without making a negative comment, and offer him an alternative that she had prepared just in case. The next day, she should offer the first vegetable again, but this time cooked in an alternative way and presented on a differently coloured plate. If that didn't work, she should keep trying by accompanying it with other foods. She should also make sure that Mark was hungry when he sat down to eat by cutting down on sugary snacks between meals.

Another suggestion was to involve Mark in choosing the vegetables they were to eat. The next time they went shopping they were to pick colourful vegetables so that they could 'cook a rainbow'.

I also asked Ann and Mark to choose some easy-to-grow vegetables, such as tomatoes, salad leaves and peas, and to plant some seeds or plants in pots or in the garden, so that Mark could have the pleasure of eating food he had grown himself.

Finally, I asked Ann to try not to appear apprehensive each time Mark sat down to eat and to treat mealtimes as normally as possible.

Mark was not an easy case at first. Ann phoned me three weeks after our consultation, saying she had tried everything I had suggested, with little or no success. I told her to persist with my methods and to try more new ways to include vegetables in Mark's diet. Slowly, Mark started to like his vegetables and even began to eat mixed salad. Ann was very pleased; her patience had paid off.

Foods to feed the brain

When we talk about good nutrition for children (and adults), we often focus on the body – the foods that help to keep the heart healthy, bones strong, joints supple and give the best resistance to diseases. The foods that feed our brain are just as important – glucose for energy, antioxidant-rich fruit and vegetables, and fats that help the brain to send the messages that keep us functioning healthily. The brain is part of the body and needs the same nourishing care.

The years between six and 10 are hugely important for your child. In the space of a few short years they will take in a vast amount of information at school. They are also learning about their place in the world, and processing the wonderful, but sometimes complex, emotions that come with families and friendship, responsibility and fun. Governing all of this is the brain, which works like a computer to control your child's body, store memories, control moods and translate the environment around them.

'The brain is part of the body and needs the same nourishing care.'

The protein-carbohydrate partnership

Brain cells require a continuous supply of oxygen and glucose – without those two nutrients, even for a few seconds, they will die. It is important to give the right carbohydrates and to team them with protein in order to keep blood sugar levels in balance. When blood sugar fluctuates, the brain's ability to function is impaired and both learning and behaviour can suffer. Complex carbohydrates help to keep sugar levels balanced and also help to carry amino acids from proteins into the brain.

A breakfast and lunch that contain complex carbohydrates and protein are the perfect way to stimulate your child's brain for the day, providing a balance of energy and the building blocks of brain chemicals to help them study. Research shows that children who eat a breakfast containing equivalent amounts of complex carbohydrates and protein learn and perform better than those that eat either a high-protein or a high-carbohydrate breakfast. Good breakfast options include low-sugar cereals such as Weetabix and Oatibix, porridge, or unsweetened natural yoghurt with fresh fruit.

Need2Know

Think-fast fats

Before your child's first birthday, their brain will have tripled in size and it will use a massive 60% of all the energy from the food they eat. Although this rate of growth slows down after the first 12 months, feeding the brain with the best food is still vitally important. This amazing organ is made mainly of fat and to keep it working well, your child needs essential fatty acids – 'essential' because the body can't make them itself. See chapter 2 for more about essential fatty acids and the foods to find them in.

Quick tip

A sandwich made with wholegrain bread and salmon, either fresh or tinned, or sardines on wholegrain toast, will make a great lunch option for your child, and they can snack on healthy seeds to keep their body and brain going throughout the day.

Fats from fried or processed foods should be eaten only in moderation, as they have a negative impact on the brain and on the health in general. Avoid foods that list 'hydrogenated' or 'partially hydrogenated' fats on the food label, as they interfere with nerve function. These dense fats may also pack blood vessels, so that less blood reaches the brain. Finally, they mean children fill up on pastries, chips, biscuits and cakes, and eat less of the foods that are naturally high in the essential fatty acids omega 3 and 6.

Let your brain breathe

The final brain-boosting ingredients in your child's diet are fresh fruit and vegetables. These are rich in vitamins C and E – powerful antioxidants that help to maintain a good supply of oxygen to the brain cells. Vitamin C is also needed to help make the brain's neurotransmitters, while vitamin B12 helps to maintain the fatty myelin sheath that protects nerve tissue. Berries, such as blueberries, are a great addition to your child's diet. Try a handful sprinkled over yoghurt or cereal for breakfast.

Food and behaviour at school

Poor concentration, restlessness, tiredness, mood swings and irritability can all be a result of low blood sugar and meals that are low in nutrients. They will affect your child's ability to learn, to enjoy school and to interact happily with fellow pupils and teachers. That's why giving your child a good breakfast to start the day and providing them with a healthy school lunch is so important.

- A study by the School Food Trust in 136 primary schools found that learning-related behaviour improved in 12 weeks when the quality of school meals and the dining room environment was improved. (Source: *School Lunch and Learning Behaviour: Primary Schools*, School Food Trust, 2007.)

- 'Eating breakfast may improve children's problem solving abilities, their memory, concentration levels, visual perception and thinking,' according to Lisa Miles, senior nutritionist at the British Nutrition Foundation. (Source: *Breakfast and Behaviour*, www.teachers.tv, accessed 2 May 2010.)

'Poor concentration, restlessness, tiredness, mood swings and irritability can all be a result of low blood sugar and meals that are low in nutrients.'

Quick tip

Don't discount school meals as a healthy option, as they are now governed by strict nutritional guidelines. Encourage your child to choose a protein food, such as chicken, fish or eggs; a carbohydrate, such as potatoes, rice or pasta; and at least one portion each of vegetables and fruit.

Quick snacks

Children have small stomachs, which means they eat smaller portions than adults. But they also need a regular supply of energy to fuel their activities. These inexpensive, delicious snacks are light enough not to spoil your child's lunch or dinner, and are much better for them than crisps and cakes.

- Miniature cheeses.

- Yoghurt with chopped fresh fruit and seeds.

- Raisins and a sliced apple.

- Rice cakes spread with hummus and served with dried apricots.
- A cup of soup or broth.
- Warm milk and home-made biscuits.

Healthy lunchboxes

Make sure that sandwich fillings are packed with goodness. Wholegrain sliced or pitta bread is the best option, but it's fine to give children white bread once or twice a week – it's all about balance. For that reason, you can pop in a biscuit, along with their fruit and vegetable snacks every now and then too.

Schools now provide fruit for a mid-morning snack. If you are at home, give your child a small apple, pear, banana, tangerine, or a few dates or dried apricots. To save time when preparing lunches, prepare some salad or vegetables when you make dinner the evening before.

Easy, nutritious lunch ideas

Cottage cheese and cucumber

Wash the cucumber and cut it into a mix of slices and sticks. Spread the cottage cheese on wholegrain bread and top with sliced cucumber. Plus, baby carrots and cucumber sticks, and two chocolate fingers.

Hummus and pitta bread

Hummus, made from chickpeas and tahini paste, is a good source of vitamins to keep your child's energy going. Add some sliced tomatoes, too.

Eggs and veg with pitta bread

If you have leftover steamed vegetables from dinner, such as spinach or broccoli, add them to pitta bread the next day with scrambled eggs. Plus, a home-made blueberry muffin.

Mozzarella or egg in a bagel with tomatoes and avocado

Slice the mozzarella and place it in the bagel. Alternatively, slice an egg you boiled the night before. Top with sliced tomatoes and avocado. Drizzle with a little olive oil. Plus, a few low-salt crisps.

Tuna, onion and watercress

Use sliced rye bread for this sandwich. Chop a small onion and two cherry tomatoes, add a tin of tuna and mix well. Spread the mixture onto the bread and top with washed and chopped watercress. Plus, a ripe pear.

Fromage frais, alfalfa and tomatoes

Spread two slices granary bread with fromage frais and top with washed alfalfa sprouts (similar to cress), slice the tomato and add.

Summing Up

- From an early age, teach your child about the wonder of foods. Let them help you choose ingredients and cook with you.

- Explain that there are no bad foods, just some we need to eat more than others.

- Experiment with different ways of serving food to encourage your child to eat more variety, but accept the occasional 'no'.

- Your child needs a balanced intake of carbohydrates and proteins, good fats, vitamins and minerals, to help brain development and functioning.

- Snack and lunch options can provide essential nutrients for your growing child, and they don't have to be difficult or expensive to prepare.

Chapter Six

Ages 11 to 18

The nutritional needs of your child will alter as they reach adolescence. Not only does a teenager need more calories to fuel their body's increased energy needs, they will require specific nutrients to support their hormonal development. Lean protein, good fats, complex carbohydrates and an adequate intake of vitamins and minerals should be part of their diet now. They have a special need for calcium and iron to help their body's development, and zinc to support the hormonal changes that occur during puberty.

A healthy diet can help your child cope with other challenges associated with the teenage years, such as skin problems, exam stress, emotional wellbeing and weight concerns. Unfortunately, this can be the time when your child decides to flex their growing independence by taking control of their own meals – and their choices may not always be high in nutritional value. They may feel the pressure to fit in with their friends by eating fast food at lunchtime, rather than the healthy lunchbox you have prepared. Skipping meals and dieting are also common. TV, magazines and the Internet will have a big influence on how they believe they should look and what they should eat.

'Calcium, iron and zinc are super-nutrients for every teenager.'

Essential nutrients for adolescents

Calcium

Essential for a range of body processes, including the formation of strong bones and teeth. A lack of calcium-rich green vegetables in the diet, as well as too many carbonated drinks that deplete calcium levels, can mean a teenager's diet is low in this important mineral.

Iron

Needed for the delivery of oxygen to every cell in the body. The most easily absorbed form of iron is found in meat. Other sources include leafy green vegetables, dried fruits and wholegrains. If your teenager's diet lacks these foods, they may be at risk of iron deficiency.

Zinc

This trace mineral boosts the immune system and is essential for healthy skin, bone growth, energy production and hormonal support. Children are very vulnerable to zinc deficiency. Low zinc levels are often associated with slow growth rate, learning problems and hyperactivity. Main sources of zinc are oysters, red meat, sardines, brazil nuts, yeast, pumpkin seeds and egg yolk.

Caring through food

Your teenager may be too busy with clubs or friends to sit down with you for lunch at the weekend, and may not want you serving a healthy casserole when mates come for dinner, but eating and sharing food with them can be a vital means of support and communication during these years. A hearty weekend breakfast can be the perfect opportunity to catch up; home-made pizzas and oven-baked fries can replace junk food; and healthy snacks can help fuel homework and calm raging emotions. Parents, carers and schools play an essential supportive role for adolescents, and offering a diet that meets their individual needs is another form of guidance and protection.

Eating tips for teens

▓ Cook at home – eating well at home can help to compensate for any fast foods your teenager chooses when they're out and about. Processed foods contain few nutrients and are high in sugar, salt, fats, chemical additives and artificial colourings. You could even ask your teenager to cook the family meal once a week.

▓ Sort out some snacks – teenagers can be reluctant to sit and eat a larger meal. Keep healthy snacks in the fridge, such as washed and chopped vegetables, yoghurt, bread sticks and hummus. Have a bowl of fruit ready to grab and go.

▓ Make healthy choices easy – replace sweetened cereal with sugar-free options, buy wholegrain bread instead of white, and serve salads with olive oil and lemon juice, instead of high-fat dressing.

▓ Teach your teenager how to read labels – weight-conscious teenagers can opt for low-fat foods that are actually high in sugar. Show them how to decode ingredient lists so they make informed choices.

▓ Be a good example – the choices you make will influence your teenager's attitude to food. Talk about, plan and enjoy meals together.

Foods for clear skin

Many teenagers have skin problems such as acne, pimples and blackheads. The cause is often a surge of hormones during puberty that stimulates oil-producing glands and/or a poor diet. The skin is the largest organ of the body and what we eat can directly affect its health. Before your teenager starts squeezing spots or spending all their money on beauty products that promise a clear complexion, get them to eat these skin-healthy foods:

▓ Oily fish – salmon, sardines and mackerel contain omega 3 fatty acids that help to protect the skin from damage. Their high protein content promotes the production of complexion-boosting collagen.

'The fast foods and sugary snacks your child eats with friends won't have such an impact if you serve healthy meals at home.'

- Dark green, leafy vegetables – packed with vitamin C, a natural antioxidant that fights skin-damaging free radicals. It also enhances iron absorption and maintains collagen levels to boost the complexion.

- Orange fruits and vegetables – apricots, pomegranates, papaya and mango are rich in vitamin A and beta carotene, which aid skin health. Carrots have been shown to have a beneficial effect on psoriasis and eczema.

- Berries – high in antioxidants and antibacterial compounds that are essential for healthy blood vessels, giving your teenager a glowing skin.

- Nuts, seeds and vegetable oils – contain vitamin E, a fat-soluble antioxidant that protects the body from free radicals and is important in skin health. Vitamin E is also found in leafy greens.

- Wholegrain bread, rice and pasta – these complex carbohydrates will satisfy your teenager's appetite, making them less likely to reach for skin-damaging sugary snacks. The good fibre they contain will also help the elimination of toxins from the body – another way to promote beautiful skin.

Emotional superfoods

Early adolescence is a period of rapid physical and mental growth. Your teenager's brain will be making new cognitive connections. The surge of hormones during puberty will change their body and impact on their emotions. At the same time, teenagers may feel under pressure to perform well at school, to earn the respect of their peers and to conform to the expectations of parents and carers.

All these demands can cause an imbalance in the body's levels of serotonin (a neurotransmitter associated with good mood and sleep), adrenalin and noradrenalin levels (neurotransmitters associated with motivation and energy). If you add a poor diet, the result can be mood swings, emotional outbursts and irritability.

Happy meal remedy – brown rice and salmon

Sugary and processed foods can cause a fast mood and energy boost. When blood sugar levels crash soon after, your teenager may feel spaced out, confused, hyperactive or irritable. Wholegrains and foods rich in omega 3 fats will boost their brainpower and happiness levels.

Happy meal remedy – turkey burgers

Tryptophan is a mood-soothing essential acid that is found in turkey, tofu, chicken, eggs and beans.

Happy meal remedy – stir-fry satay chicken with greens

B vitamins support the nervous system, boost learning ability and energy, and help to reduce stress. Find them in wholegrains, green leafy vegetables and nuts, including peanuts.

Hormone helpers

The adolescent years mark the transition from childhood to early adulthood and it is hormones that make that change possible. Adding the nutrients listed below to an already balanced diet will assist this rapid physical and emotional growth spurt. This spurt generally happens between the ages of 10 and 13 for girls and 12 to 15 for boys. Poor nutrition at this stage can affect growth and delay sexual development.

- Macronutrients (see chapter 2) are needed, particularly by boys, to fuel their increase in muscle mass and body size.
- Vitamin B for energy metabolism.
- Iron for preventing anaemia. This is especially important for girls when they start their period.
- Calcium and vitamin D have an impact on hormone secretion, and help

'If you are extremely worried about your teenager's happiness or mental wellbeing, consult your GP or another health professional.'

to increase the density and growth of bones. Vitamin D, as well as being obtained from foods such as butter, margarine, oily fish and fortified cereals, is produced in the body during exposure to sunlight.

- Iodine is needed to support the thyroid – find it in seafood, seaweed and iodised salt.

- Zinc is essential for protein synthesis and the activity of several enzymes.

- Vitamins A, C and E are beneficial to newly synthesised cells. Vitamin C also supports the endocrine system, which is responsible for the release of some hormones.

Exam menus

Exam time can put particular stress on your teenager. Long hours spent revising may mean they reach for sugary snacks and caffeine for a quick-fix energy boost. Breakfast and lunch can be missed as they rush out the door to the exam hall. As a parent or carer, you can help to take the strain out of mealtimes by planning a menu of exam-friendly options. If your teenager is eating foods that help to boost their energy, focus and emotional wellbeing, they're one step closer to success.

- Plan all meals for the week ahead, choosing nutritious foods to boost your teenager's health and performance – include foods that contain essential fatty acids, zinc, B vitamins, iron, calcium and folic acid every day (see chapter 2).

- Buy a stock of fresh fruit and vegetables for meals and snacks.

- Minimise sugary foods because they suppress the immune system.

- Eating too much animal protein in the same day may overload the digestive system. Try to make one meal an easily digested vegetable soup or pulses with rice.

- Make sure your teenager doesn't skip breakfast, as this will provide fuel for body and mind during the day ahead.

Exam week menu ideas

Breakfast

Porridge with blueberries, a tablespoon of mixed seeds and a teaspoon of wheatgerm.

Plain yoghurt with blueberries or a sliced banana, and one teaspoon of mixed seeds.

Toast with avocado or an egg.

Morning snack

Fruit, yoghurt, rice cake with hummus, seeds or almonds.

Lunch and dinner

Salmon, mackerel or sea bass with broccoli and carrots.

Chicken or turkey with carrots and sweet potatoes.

Freshly made vegetable soup, such as leek, potatoes and carrot soup with organic brown rice.

Rice with cooked vegetables and chicken.

Cod with potato and mixed vegetables.

Fish with green beans.

Turkey with runner beans and sweet potatoes.

Drinks

Filtered water or diluted fresh fruit juices. Avoid fizzy drinks and squash as they are high in sugar and artificial additives.

Eating disorders

The leading UK eating disorders charity, beat, estimates that there are 1.15 million people in the UK with diagnosed and undiagnosed eating disorders, including anorexia (restriction of food) and bulimia (binge eating followed by vomiting, taking laxatives, exercise and/or food restriction, in order not to gain weight). Young people between the ages of 12 and 25 are most likely to be affected by eating disorders, and the problem affects girls more than boys – it's estimated that 10% of all cases of eating disorders are male. (Source: www.b-eat.co.uk, accessed 23 May 2010).

It's thought that eating disorders are most often caused by a combination of factors including traumatic events, such as divorce or bereavement; low self-esteem; difficult relationships with family or friends; problems at school; illness; and abuse. An individual's genetic make-up and the influence of the media may also play their part. Whatever the cause, the effect of not eating is simple and dangerous – malnutrition. This can cause long-term health problems such as heart, kidney and digestive problems, infertility and osteoporosis. If you have any concerns about your teenager's eating habits and attitude to food, consult your GP or a specialist in eating disorders.

'If you suspect your teenager may have an eating disorder, consult your GP for more advice.'

Obesity

The number of overweight and obese children and young people is a cause for concern. According to figures from the NHS, 20.6% of 11 to 15-year-old boys and 18.3% of 11 to 15-year-old girls in England in 2008 were obese. (Source: *Statistics on Obesity, Physical Activity and Diet: England, 2010*, www.ic.nhs.uk, accessed 7 September 2010.)

As a parent or carer, you may be concerned about how much your teenager eats. But it's important to remember that adolescence is a period of rapid growth and development, and that will naturally result in increased appetite. Your teenager needs a store of energy to fuel the physical changes that happen to their body during puberty. The challenge is to provide a diet that will support this growth spurt without providing excess calories. You may also need to encourage your teenager to take part in physical activities that will help them to manage their weight and promote good health, as well as providing relaxation and social opportunities.

Triggers for overeating

Emotional upset, stress and sugar imbalances – all common teenage experiences – can trigger a response in the hypothalamus in the brain that causes us to reach for food. The temptation is to turn to 'comfort' foods that are high in sugar and fat, which stimulate a feel-good emotional response in the brain and provide an instant hit of energy. Unfortunately this makes matters worse as the energy given is quickly burnt, making us want to eat more of the same food again. The result is a diet high in calories that are stored as fat in the body.

Talking to your teenager about weight

- Raise the matter carefully – showing too much anxiety, putting them on a diet or being overly critical may cause a loss of confidence or disordered eating in your teenager.

- Explain what your concerns are and suggest ways your teenager might eat more healthily.

- Remember your child is an individual – there is no set limit on how much a teenager should eat. Look carefully at their diet, lifestyle and activity levels before assuming they eat too much.

- If you feel your child's diet is healthy, you may want to encourage them to be more active. This doesn't have to mean sport – street dancing, skateboarding and walking will all burn energy.

- Give your teenager time. You may find that weight gain is followed by a growth spurt that balances their ratio of weight to height again.

The no-diet diet

Simple changes to what your teenager (and the whole family) eats can boost their wellbeing and result in weight loss without dieting.

- Opt for simple, natural seasoning for salads or vegetables, such as extra virgin olive oil and lemon or cider vinegar. These will be healthier and contain fewer calories than bought salad dressing or mayonnaise.

- Increase the amount of vegetables your teenager eats. Include orange, yellow and green options for good vitamin and mineral input.

- Don't serve highly-salted food and preserved meat. High-salt foods can cause cravings that may cause your teenager to eat more.

- Spend time reading labels before buying foods. Be aware that some low-fat foods have large amounts of sugar in them.

- Avoid processed ready meals and takeaways, which have more calories than natural whole foods.

- Allow occasional treats. Encourage your teenager to eat something healthy before going out with friends, to reduce the risk of overeating. Encourage them to get back to eating healthily afterwards.

- Eat well as a family and talk openly about why you've chosen the food on the table.

- Get active – the whole family can benefit from physical activity, which increases the amount of energy consumed by the body, as well as having health benefits. Weight is lost when we burn more energy than we consume, as the body uses fat deposits for fuel.

- Actively enjoy food.

- Mindful eating – when we really think about what we put in our mouths – has been shown to reduce calorie intake. If your teenager must snack as they surf the Internet, provide healthier options such as rice cakes, vegetable sticks and toasted seeds.

Case study: the overweight teenager

Cinzia was 18 and came to see me because she was obese and wanted advice on how to improve her diet. Her GP had examined her and concluded she didn't have any underlying health problems that were causing her to put on weight. His recommendation was to eat less and exercise more. Cinzia confessed to me that she did every diet around with poor results – after a few months the weight, and more, would go back on. She felt unhappy and hungry all the time.

I told Cinzia that if she ate a good, balanced diet for 80% of the time, she could afford to indulge in what I call 'socialising' foods for the remaining 20%. I asked her to limit the amount of calorie-dense, high sugar and fat foods she ate. Instead of starting the day with a breakfast of white bread, butter and jam, she should eat wholegrains such as oats, wheat or rice with added seeds and fruit. This would keep her blood sugar level in balance for longer. For dinner, I suggested she swap white pasta and cream sauces for wholegrain varieties with a simple tomato sauce, and eat baked potatoes or potatoes roasted in a little olive oil instead of chips, with lean protein and lots of vegetables. Snacks should be fruit and crackers, rather than sweets and crisps.

To encourage her, I asked her to keep a food diary that recorded her emotions as well as what she ate. She soon came to realise that her overeating was triggered by anxiety – if she felt pressured at school or by her peers, she turned to food. As Cinzia enjoyed walking, I asked her to go out for a walk whenever she felt tense and tempted to reach for the biscuit barrel. Three months later Cinzia had reached a healthy weight for her body type and had also developed healthy ways to ease stress.

'A diet can restrict an adolescent's supply of nutrients just when they need them most. It's best to look at what they eat, not how much.'

Summing Up

- Adolescents have specific nutritional needs to support the rapid growth and development of the body.

- A healthy diet at home can help to compensate for poor food choices elsewhere.

- Teenage skin problems can be improved with foods that help to care for the complexion.

- Certain ingredients contain natural elements that can help to calm mood swings.

- Eating foods rich in particular nutrients can help the development of hormones during puberty.

- You can plan menus to support your teenager during exam periods.

- Young people between the ages of 12 and 25 are most at risk of developing eating disorders.

- Family support and simple dietary changes can help to tackle the continuing problem of teenage obesity and overeating.

Chapter Seven

Purées and First Foods

Preparing your child's first purées and gradually introducing them to solid food is an incredibly exciting time. It's a delight to watch them discover new tastes and textures, even if your carefully planned menus end up on the floor sometimes! First foods aren't just about flavour, though. What you give your child to eat in this first year can help to establish healthy eating patterns for life – it helps to instil an appreciation of fresh, nutritious produce; to teach manners and how to eat well; and to show that shared meals can be a special time for all the family.

See chapter 3 for the basics of how to choose, prepare and cook food in the first year, and try out some of the recipes in this chapter. With quick, inexpensive and foolproof options like these, you won't need to rely on processed jars of baby food.

'Preparing your child's first purées and gradually introducing them to solid food is an incredibly exciting time.'

Purées

First-food purées are simply peeled fruit and vegetables that are steamed or boiled then mashed – choose avocado and banana and you don't even have to cook them first. Start by serving just one type of food at a time. As your child gets used to eating these, mix them into tempting mouthfuls that provide interesting tastes and essential nutrients.

Remember that preparing your child's food doesn't have to be a hassle – you can simply set aside some of the unseasoned, cooked vegetables you have prepared for your meal and whiz them in a blender or mouli to make a purée. Keep some of the cooking water, or use cooled boiled water, to thin the mixture if necessary.

Try these combinations – you can experiment with the balance of flavours or mix and match ingredients, depending on your child's tastes and what's in season.

- Pea and mint.

- Pea and carrot.

- Broccoli and cauliflower.

- Carrot and cauliflower.

- Broccoli with mashed potato.

- Butternut squash and pear.

- Butternut squash and sweet potato.

- Apple and cinnamon.

- Apple and pear, with mashed banana.

- Kiwi and melon.

- Pear and plum with cinnamon.

A note on the recipes

- All recipes make around six child portions, unless it states otherwise. Any food that isn't eaten immediately can be divided into portions, cooled and kept in the fridge for up to 24 hours, or frozen.

- Recipes containing only fruits or vegetables can be frozen for up to six months. Recipes with milk can be frozen for up to four weeks. Recipes with fish or meat can be frozen for up to 10 weeks.

- Don't add salt or sugar, unless specified.

- Use full-fat milk. Avoid dairy products if your child is allergic or sensitive to them.

- Choose free-range, organic eggs and organic milk if possible, as they have more nutrients.

- Wash all vegetables before cooking, scrubbing them with a brush to remove dirt and residues, if necessary.

- You can increase the quantities and cook many of the recipes for all the family. Simply season at the end of cooking, once you have removed your child's portion from the pan.

Seven to nine months

You can now start introducing protein to your child's diet – chicken, turkey, white fish and lentils are easy to digest.

Chicken and Rice Casserole Purée

The combination of chicken, carrot and rice is mild and sweet tasting. This meal is packed with nutrients, including beta carotene, vitamin A and protein.

Ingredients
50g wholegrain rice
300ml water
100g chicken breast, skinned and cut into strips
1 small carrot, peeled and chopped
150g sweet potato, peeled and chopped
50g peas, fresh or frozen

Method
1. Put the rice, water, chicken, carrot and sweet potato into a saucepan over a high heat. Bring to the boil, lower the heat and simmer for around 30 minutes.
2. Add the peas and cook for another 5 minutes, or until the chicken is cooked and the vegetables are tender.
3. Whiz in a blender, adding a little boiled water to thin the purée if necessary.

Turkey and Tomato Purée

Turkey is a rich source of protein, zinc, B vitamins and iron – superb nutrients for boosting your child's immunity.

Ingredients

1 tbsp extra virgin olive oil
25g onion, peeled and chopped
100g carrot, peeled and chopped
100g potato, peeled and chopped
1 small turkey breast, cut into strips
200g fresh tomatoes, peeled, deseeded and chopped, or tinned tomatoes
150ml water

Method

1. Put the olive oil in a saucepan over a medium heat. Add the onion and carrot and sauté until softened.
2. Add the potato and turkey and sauté for another 5 minutes.
3. Add the tomatoes and water, bring the mixture to the boil and then simmer for 30 minutes, until the turkey is cooked and the potato is soft.
4. Whiz in a blender, adding a little boiled water to thin the purée if necessary.

Squash and Lentil Purée

Red lentils are rich in protein and iron, and easy for young children to digest.

Ingredients

1 tbsp extra virgin olive oil
25g onion, peeled and chopped
100g carrot, peeled and chopped
200g butternut squash, peeled and cut into chunks
50g red lentils
400ml water
1 tsp fresh parsley, chopped

Method

1. Put the olive oil in a saucepan over a medium heat. Add the onion and carrot and sauté until softened.
2. Add the butternut squash, lentils, water and parsley. Bring the mixture to the boil, then cover and simmer for 25 minutes until the squash is tender.
3. Whiz in a blender, adding a little boiled water to thin the purée if necessary.

Italian Vegetable Pasta

Tomatoes and red pepper are rich in beta carotene, which helps to support the immune system. Use mini pasta shapes, made for soup, in this recipe.

Ingredients
200g fresh tomatoes, peeled, deseeded and chopped, or tinned tomatoes
1 red pepper, chopped
1 small courgette, chopped
175ml water
25g mini pasta shapes

Method
1. Put the tomatoes, pepper, courgette and water in a saucepan over a medium heat. Bring to the boil, cover and then simmer for 15 minutes.
2. Whiz the sauce in a blender until smooth.
3. Put the pasta in a pan of boiling water and cook for 5-7 minutes, until soft.
4. Stir the pasta into the sauce and serve.

Plaice and Tomato Pasta

A rich source of calcium, protein and antioxidant vitamins to protect your child's immune defences.

Ingredients

1 fillet of plaice, skinned
1 tsp extra virgin olive oil
150g fresh tomatoes, skinned, deseeded and chopped, or tinned tomatoes
150ml milk
25g mini pasta shapes

Method

1. Preheat the oven to 180°C/350°F/Gas Mark 4.
2. Put the plaice into an ovenproof dish, drizzle with the olive oil and cover with the tomatoes. Pour over the milk. Cover the dish with a lid or foil and bake in the oven for 20 minutes, until the fish is cooked.
3. Meanwhile, put the pasta in a pan of boiling water and cook for 5-7 minutes, until soft.
4. Mash the fish and tomatoes together, stir in the pasta and serve.

'Pick and mix – replace the pasta with mashed potato.'

Cod and Corn Chowder

This dish contains vitamin B12, potassium and selenium, and is a great source of energy.

Ingredients
100g cod fillet, skinned and bones removed
300ml milk
75g sweet potato or butternut squash, chopped
50g frozen sweetcorn

Method
1. Put the fish and milk in a saucepan and cook over a medium heat for 7 minutes. Remove the fish from the pan, reserving the milk.
2. Add the sweet potato or butternut squash to the pan with the milk. Bring to the boil, and then simmer for 10 minutes. Add the sweetcorn and cook for another 5 minutes.
3. Flake the fish and add to the milk and vegetables. Whiz in a blender and serve.

'Pick and mix – use any other white fish instead of cod.'

Nine to 12 months

Your child will be able to eat many of the same foods you do now, so share these recipe ideas with them and enjoy mealtimes together whenever possible.

Spinach and Lentil Purée

A good source of iron and protein.

Ingredients
180g red lentils
1 tbsp extra virgin olive oil
1 small onion, chopped
1 tsp mild curry powder
180g frozen spinach
125ml coconut milk

Method
1. Put the lentils in a saucepan, cover with water and cook over a medium heat for 20 minutes until tender. Drain away the water when cooked.
2. Put the olive oil in a saucepan over a medium heat. Add the onion and cook for 5 minutes until softened.
3. Stir the curry powder into the onions and cook for 2-3 minutes.
4. Add the spinach, lentils and coconut milk, bring to the boil and then simmer for 10 minutes.
5. Purée before serving, if necessary.

'Pick and mix – swap the lentils for cooked chickpeas.'

Crispy Courgette and Carrot Bake

Oats make a tasty topping that provides slow-release energy and vital nutrients.

Ingredients

250g courgettes, grated
250g carrots, grated
1 small onion, finely chopped
1 tsp lemon juice

For the topping:
50g rolled oats
4 tsp extra virgin olive oil
25g Parmesan cheese, grated

Method

1. Preheat the oven to 180°C/350°F/Gas Mark 4.
2. Put the courgettes, carrots, onion and lemon juice in a bowl and mix well. Put the mixture into an ovenproof dish.
3. Put the oats into a bowl, pour over the oil and mix well. Stir in the cheese.
4. Sprinkle the oats over the courgette and carrot mixture. Bake in the oven for 25 minutes, until the vegetables are soft and the topping is crisp and golden.

Cheesy Salmon and Spinach

Oily fish such as salmon helps to support brain development.

Ingredients
200g salmon fillet
25g butter
175g frozen spinach

For the sauce:
25g butter
2 tbsp plain flour
175ml milk
50g mild Cheddar cheese

Method
1. Preheat the oven to 180°C/350°F/Gas Mark 4.
2. Put the salmon in an ovenproof dish and dot with butter. Cover with a lid or foil and bake for 8-10 minutes, until cooked.
3. Put the spinach in a saucepan with 2 tbsp water. Cook over a medium heat until heated through. Drain and squeeze excess water from the spinach.
4. To make the sauce, put the butter in a saucepan and melt over a low heat. Remove from the heat and stir in the flour to make a paste. Gradually add the milk, stirring continuously. When the sauce is combined, return to the heat and add the cheese. Stir until the cheese is melted.
5. Put the spinach on a plate, flake over the salmon, drizzle with cheese sauce, and serve.

Fish Pie

A meal all the family can enjoy. The fish and potato is a good combination of protein and carbohydrate.

Ingredients

150g cod fillet, skinned and cut into chunks
150g salmon fillet, skinned and cut into chunks
300ml milk
1 bay leaf
1 small onion, chopped
25g butter
25g plain flour
1 tbsp fresh parsley, chopped

For the topping:
300g potatoes, peeled and chopped
100g carrots, peeled and chopped
25g butter
2 tbsp milk

Method

1. Preheat the oven to 180°C/350°F/Gas Mark 4.
2. Put the fish, milk, bay leaf and onion in a saucepan over a medium heat. Bring to the boil and then simmer for 8 minutes until the fish is cooked. Remove the fish, then strain and reserve the milk and discard the onions and bayleaf.
3. Melt the butter in a saucepan over a medium heat. Stir in the flour to make a paste. Gradually add the reserved milk, stirring continuously to make a smooth sauce.
4. Flake the fish and stir it into the sauce with the parsley. Pour into an ovenproof dish.
5. Meanwhile, put the potatoes and carrots into a saucepan, cover with water, bring to the boil and then simmer for 15-20 minutes until soft. Drain and then mash with the butter and milk.
6. Top the fish mixture with the potato and carrot mash. Bake for 15-20 minutes until golden.

Lamb and Lentil Stew

Rich in protein and fibre. This tasty stew is rich in protein and fibre. Adding inexpensive lentils to the recipe means using less lamb too.

Ingredients

200g lean lamb, trimmed and cut into cubes
50g red lentils
200g sweet potato, peeled and chopped
1 tsp tomato purée
350ml water

Method

1. Put all the ingredients into a saucepan over a medium heat. Bring to the boil and then simmer for 30-35 minutes, stirring occasionally, until the lamb and lentils are soft.
2. If necessary, purée or mash the stew before serving.

Beef Casserole

A filling and delicious mix of nutritious vegetables and protein-rich beef.

Ingredients

2 tbsp extra virgin olive oil
350g braising beef, trimmed and cut into cubes
1 clove garlic, chopped
1 onion, chopped
2 sticks of celery, chopped
2 carrots, chopped
1 tbsp plain flour
600ml water
2 tsp mixed dried herbs
1 tbsp tomato purée
200g mushrooms, chopped
450g potatoes, peeled and chopped

Method

1. Preheat the oven to 170°C/325°F/Gas Mark 3.
2. Put 1 tbsp olive oil into a casserole dish, add the beef and sauté over a medium heat, until browned. Remove from the pan and reserve.
3. Put the remaining 1 tbsp olive into the casserole dish, add the garlic and onion and sauté over a medium heat for 5 minutes until softened. Add the celery and carrots and cook for another 5 minutes.
4. Return the beef to the dish. Sprinkle over the flour and stir in. Gradually stir in the water, then add the herbs and tomato purée. Bring to the boil and stir until the sauce starts to thicken.
5. Cover the casserole dish, transfer to the oven and cook for 1½ hours.
6. Add the mushrooms and potatoes and cook for another 30-40 minutes, until the meat and potatoes are soft.
7. Purée or mash the casserole, if necessary, before serving.

Scones with blueberries or sultanas

A special treat for children and adults. The fruit adds fibre and vitamins to the tasty scones.

Makes about 8

Ingredients
225g self-raising flour
1 tsp baking powder
50g unsalted butter, cut into pieces
50g sugar
1 egg, beaten
100ml milk
50g fresh frozen blueberries, or sultanas

Method
1. Preheat the oven to 230°C/gas mark 8.
2. Sift the flour and baking powder into a mixing bowl and rub in the butter until the mixture is like breadcrumbs. Add the blueberries or sultanas and stir through the mixture.
3. Add the sugar, egg and milk and mix to form a soft dough.
4. Turn the dough on to a floured surface and knead lightly. Roll out to about 1cm thick and cut into rounds.
5. Bake for around 10 minutes, until risen and golden.

Summing Up

- First foods introduce new tastes and textures to your child.

- Home-made meals can be more economical than processed foods.

- Cooking dishes for your child means you can choose fresh, seasonal and nutritious ingredients, with no added chemicals or artificial flavourings.

- Choosing healthy food options from the start can help to establish good eating habits for life.

- Sharing meals as a family can be a special time together, and can help your child to learn social skills.

Chapter Eight
Good Start Breakfasts

A good breakfast is a fantastic source of nutrients and will help your child to meet each day feeling healthy, strong and full of energy. Of course, in the rush to get up and get ready for playgroup, school, or just the day ahead, it's easy to reach for the sugary cereal you know your child won't refuse. But the recipes below are quick to prepare, full of goodness and children love them.

We've even included simple smoothies for children who don't like to eat too much first thing. Remember, a poor breakfast or no breakfast will have an effect on your child's school performance and, in the long run, on their body's overall nutritional balance.

A note on the recipes

- All recipes serve four, unless it states otherwise.

- Use full-fat milk if your child is five years or younger; semi-skimmed if older.

- Choose free-range, organic eggs and organic milk if possible, as they have more nutrients.

- Wash all vegetables before cooking, scrubbing them with a brush to remove dirt and residues, if necessary.

- Don't add salt or sugar, unless specified.

Fruity Porridge

This tasty porridge is a great source of slow-release energy, to sustain your child until lunch. Oats contain B vitamins, carbohydrates, protein, fibre and essential minerals. Milk provides calcium and vitamins A and D, and apples and blueberries are packed with antioxidants and vitamins.

Ingredients
200g rolled oats
200ml milk
400ml hot water
2 ripe apples, peeled and grated
1 tsp ground cinnamon
Handful blueberries, to serve

'Pick and mix – you could also use millet flakes or brown rice flakes instead of oats.'

Method
1. Put all the ingredients except the blueberries in a saucepan over a low heat.
2. Stir continuously for around 5 minutes, until the liquid is absorbed and the oats are soft.
3. Serve with a handful of blueberries.

Boosted Oatibix

This contains all the goodness of the oats, plus yoghurt containing vitamins B2 and B12, calcium, magnesium and bacteria cultures. The seeds and wheatgerm are packed with more fantastic nutrients. As the energy in the breakfast is released slowly, it will help to keep your child's blood sugar levels in balance.

Ingredients
2 tbsp plain yoghurt
Milk, to cover
4 bowls of Oatibix flakes
75g wheatgerm
2 tbsp mixed seeds, such as sesame, sunflower and pumpkin
2 tbsp almonds, chopped
500g fresh fruit, chopped

Method
1. Add the yoghurt and milk to the bowls of Oatibix.
2. Add the wheatgerm, mixed seeds, almonds and fresh fruit, then serve.

'Bought boxes of cereal can be a good choice for kids, as they contain B vitamins, iron, calcium and other essential nutrients. Choose varieties that are low in sugar and salt.'

Cheesy Omelette

Serve eggs with a slice of wholemeal bread – the combination of protein and carbohydrate will give a slow release of energy for several hours. Eggs contain complete proteins, while wholemeal bread provides vitamins B and E. Serve with a glass of orange juice on the side – the vitamin C content will help to protect your child from cold viruses.

Serves 2

'Pick and mix – mix it up by adding tomatoes, spinach or goat's cheese as an alternative to Cheddar. Or serve poached or scrambled eggs instead of an omelette.'

Ingredients
4 eggs
4 tbsp milk
25g mild Cheddar cheese, grated
Knob of unsalted butter or a little extra virgin olive oil
4 slices wholemeal bread, toasted, or wholemeal pitta bread

Method
1. Whisk the eggs and milk in a jug, and stir in the cheese.
2. Melt the butter or heat the oil in a pan over a medium heat.
3. Pour in the egg mixture and cook until set.
4. Serve the omelette on the toast or inside the pitta bread.

Bio-yoghurt with Seeds and Berries

A light breakfast that's good when your child is in a hurry or just wants a change from cereal. The berries and seeds are full of nutrients, and the bacteria in the yoghurt will help digestion.

Serves 1

Ingredients
1 pot of plain yoghurt
1 tbsp mixed seeds (sesame, pumpkin and sunflower)
1 tbsp flaked almonds
Handful of berries (raspberries, strawberries, blackberries or blueberries)

Method
1. Place the yoghurt in a small bowl and top with the seeds, almonds and berries.

Oatmeal Toast with Avocado

Avocado contains B vitamins, carotenoids, potassium, folic acid, zinc and omega 6 fatty acids. Serve this with a glass of milk for a great start to the day.

Serves 1

Ingredients
2 slices of oatmeal bread, toasted
½ avocado
A squeeze of lemon juice, to taste

Method
1. Mash the avocado then spread it with a fork on top of the bread. Add a squeeze of lemon juice, if desired.

'For an extra serving of essential fatty acids, potassium and antioxidants, add mixed seeds and a handful of blueberries or a sliced ripe banana, then serve with milk.'

Banana Smoothie

Bananas are full of potassium, while the natural yoghurt contains natural bacteria that will help to soothe your child's tummy after upsets.

Ingredients
25g rolled oats or 1 Weetabix
125ml milk
1 small banana
1 pot of natural yoghurt or more, to taste

Method
1. Put the oats or Weetabix into a blender and pour over the milk. Leave to soak for about 5 minutes.
2. Add the banana and yoghurt and whiz until blended. Serve immediately.

Tropical Smoothie

Slow-release energy, soluble fibre, plus vitamin E – not to mention the yummy taste – make this a winner for children.

Serves 1

Ingredients
1 ripe papaya or mango
2 bananas
150ml water

Method
1. Whiz all the ingredients in a blender until smooth and serve.

Breakfast Pancakes

A lovely weekend treat. The fresh berries provide antioxidants and the wholemeal flour contains fibre to help your child feel fuller for longer.

Makes 10 pancakes

Ingredients
125g wholemeal flour
2 eggs
200ml milk
90ml water
60g butter or olive oil
Strawberries, raspberries and blueberries, to serve
Runny honey or maple syrup, to serve

Method
1. Sift the flour into a bowl, break in both eggs and whisk together.
2. Combine the milk and water in a jug, then whisk into the egg mixture a little at a time to make a smooth batter.
3. Melt half the butter and stir into the batter or add half the olive oil.
4. Melt the remaining butter in a frying pan over a medium heat, or use olive oil, if preferred. Add a small ladleful of batter – just enough to coat the base of the pan in a thin layer.
5. Cook the pancake for around 1 minute, then use a spatula to flip it over. Cook for another minute.
6. Put the pancake on a plate, top with a handful of fruit and a drizzle of honey or maple syrup.
7. Continue until you have used all the batter.

'Pick and mix – in winter, serve the pancakes with a warm compote of prunes and apricots that have been chopped and softened in a saucepan with 2 tbsp apple juice.'

Summing Up

▪ A healthy breakfast will give your child energy for the day ahead and give them a good nutritional balance in the long term.

▪ Fresh fruit and seeds can be added to commercial cereals to increase their nutrient content.

▪ A combination of protein and carbohydrates will help to maintain energy levels for longer.

▪ Smoothies are a good option if your child doesn't like to eat a large breakfast.

Chapter Nine

Keep Going Lunches

Chapter 5 has ideas for healthy sandwich options for your child's lunchbox, but sometimes you want to serve more than sandwiches in the middle of the day, especially at the weekend when the whole family may have more time to eat together. Meals that include protein as well as carbohydrates are good choices as they will help to keep your child's blood sugar levels stable, giving them plenty of energy for the afternoon's activities.

Of course, many children will eat lunches provided by their school during the week rather than taking in their own food. In that case, talking to your child about the goodness that different types of food provide can help them to pick the best options for a well-balanced plateful.

Tagliatelle with Ham

This pasta dish is quick to prepare and the combination of carbohydrates from the pasta and protein in the cheese and ham provides lots of slow-release energy.

Serves 4-6

Ingredients
500g egg tagliatelle
2 tbsp extra virgin olive oil and a knob of butter
2 cloves garlic, finely sliced
200g prosciutto, or other ham, sliced
200g peas, cooked
2 tbsp Parmesan cheese, grated

'Pick and mix – use inexpensive salmon offcuts, available from supermarkets, instead of the prosciutto.'

Method
1. Cook the tagliatelle following the packet instructions, then drain and put into a serving bowl.
2. Meanwhile, put the olive oil and butter in a saucepan over a medium heat. Add the garlic, prosciutto and peas and warm through.
3. Add the ham and peas mixture to the tagliatelle and toss together. Sprinkle over the Parmesan and serve.

Steak with Tomatoes

This dish contains a broad variety of nutrients that a growing child needs, especially iron and zinc.

Serves 4

Ingredients
2-3 tbsp extra virgin olive oil
4 fillet steaks
4 cloves garlic, chopped
1 small onion, chopped
Pinch of salt
8 large ripe tomatoes, peeled, deseeded and chopped
4 tbsp fresh parsley, chopped
Steamed broccoli, to serve

Method
1. Put the oil in a frying pan over a medium heat. Add the steaks, garlic and onion. Cook the steak for around 4 minutes on each side, until brown.
2. When the meat is cooked, remove it from the pan and place it on a warm plate. Season the steaks with a pinch of salt and cover with another plate, to keep warm.
3. Add the tomatoes to the frying pan, squash them gently with a fork and cook over a low heat until they form a thick sauce.
4. Return the steaks to the pan with the tomatoes. Add the chopped parsley and cook for a further 5 minutes.
5. Serve with steamed broccoli on the side.

'Pick and mix – swap the steak for turkey escalopes for a milder and more economical version of this dish.'

Quick Pasta

Children love the mild taste of courgettes cooked in yoghurt or cream.

Serves 4

Ingredients
2 tbsp extra virgin olive oil
1 onion, chopped
4 medium courgettes, diced
60ml plain yoghurt or cream
Knob of butter
400g spaghetti
Grated Parmesan to serve, according to taste.

Method
1. Put the oil in a saucepan over a medium heat. Add the onion and cook until softened.
2. Add the courgettes to the pan and cook for 5 minutes over a low heat until softened.
3. Add the yoghurt or cream to the pan with a knob of butter. Gently heat through for 3-4 minutes.
4. Meanwhile, cook the spaghetti following the packet instructions, then drain. Toss the spaghetti in the courgette sauce and serve immediately, sprinkled with Parmesan.

Mushrooms and Rice

Mushrooms contain many of the same nutrients as meat, without the saturated fats. This meal is rich in iron, B vitamins, carbohydrates and protein.

Serves 4

Ingredients
400g wholegrain rice
4 tbsp extra virgin olive oil
1 small onion, peeled and finely chopped
15 button mushrooms, wiped and finely sliced
Salt and freshly ground black pepper
2 tbsp fresh parsley, chopped

Method
1. Boil a pan of water, add the rice and simmer for around 30 minutes, until cooked. Then drain, reserving a little of the cooking water.
2. Meanwhile, put the oil in a large saucepan over a medium heat. Add the onion and mushrooms and sauté for 10 minutes. Season the mushrooms with a little salt and black pepper.
3. Lower the heat and add the cooked rice and a ladleful of the reserved cooking water to the pan. Heat gently until all water is absorbed, stirring occasionally.
4. Serve in a bowl garnished with the chopped parsley.

Lentil and Potato Soup

This is a 'complete' meal, with the perfect balance of proteins, carbohydrates and iron.

Serves 4-6

Ingredients
350g brown lentils
4 tbsp olive oil
2 cloves garlic, chopped
1 small onion, peeled and finely chopped
2 slices bacon, fat removed
1 tin of tomatoes or 4 ripe tomatoes, sliced
3 medium white potatoes, chopped
2 carrots, sliced
Salt and freshly ground black pepper
2 slices wholemeal bread, crusts removed and cut into cubes

Method
1. Soak the lentils overnight. Then when ready to cook, rinse the lentils in cold water several times.
2. Put 1 tbsp oil in a saucepan over a medium heat. Add the garlic, onion and bacon, and cook for 5 minutes.
3. Add the tomatoes, lentils, chopped potatoes and enough water to cover (add more water if needed later). Season the soup. Cover and cook for around 35 minutes, until the lentils and potatoes are tender.
4. Heat the remaining 3 tbsp oil in a frying pan over a medium heat. Fry the bread until golden to make croutons. Remove from the pan and drain on kitchen paper. Sprinkle onto the soup and serve.

Delicious Salmon

Children love the pink salmon and colourful vegetables in this dish. It is rich in essential fatty acids and vitamins.

Serves 4

Ingredients
4 salmon steaks
4 cloves garlic, chopped
1 parsnip, peeled and cut into sticks
1 courgette, sliced
6 pitted black olives, halved
6 cherry tomatoes, halved
4 carrots, peeled and cut into sticks
1 sweet potato, peeled and diced
Pinch of salt
4 tbsp extra virgin olive oil
2 tbsp fresh parsley, chopped

Method
1. Preheat the oven to 210°C/410°F/Gas Mark 7.
2. Put the salmon steaks in an ovenproof dish and place the vegetables around them.
3. Season the fish and drizzle with the olive oil. Add 4 tbsp water and bake in the oven for 40 minutes until the fish flakes and the vegetables are tender.
4. Remove from the oven, sprinkle with parsley and serve.

'Pick and mix – use cod instead of salmon, if you prefer, and choose whatever vegetables are in season.'

Tortellini with Ricotta Sauce

Soft, sweet ricotta makes a delicious alternative to the usual cheese sauces. A good mix of protein and carbohydrate.

Serves 4

Ingredients
3 tbsp extra virgin olive oil
500g ripe tomatoes or tinned tomatoes
Small bunch fresh basil leaves, torn
Pinch of salt
500g tortellini pasta
300g ricotta
2 tbsp Parmesan cheese, grated

Method
1. Put the oil in a saucepan over a medium heat. Add the tomatoes, basil and salt and cook for 20-30 minutes.
2. Cook the tortellini following the packet instructions, and drain.
3. Sieve the ricotta and pour it into the warm sauce. Stir to combine.
4. Add the cooked tortellini and mix well.
5. Divide into bowls, sprinkle with Parmesan and serve.

Smoked Haddock Kedgeree

Protein from the fish and fibre and wholegrain carbohydrates from the rice combine to make a satisfying brunch or lunch dish. Smoked foods can be high in salt, so it's best not to serve them too frequently.

Ingredients
300g undyed smoked haddock
2 eggs
500ml water
200g wholegrain rice
2 cloves garlic, sliced
2 tbsp fresh parsley, chopped
1 pot natural yoghurt

Method
1. Put the fish in a saucepan with 2-3 tbsp water. Cover and cook over a medium heat for around 8 minutes, until the fish flakes and is cooked through.
2. Hard boil the eggs, peel and chop.
3. Put 500ml water in a saucepan and bring to the boil. Add the rice and garlic, stir, then reduce the heat and cover with a lid. Simmer for around 25-30 minutes, until the rice is cooked and all the water is absorbed.
4. Stir the cooked haddock, egg, parsley and yoghurt into the rice and serve.

Home-made Fish Fingers

The goodness of oats and fish in one perfect package for children.

Ingredients

350g cod or haddock, cut into strips
25g wholemeal breadcrumbs
25g oat flakes
1 egg
2 tbsp extra virgin olive oil or sunflower oil
Salad or green vegetables, to serve

Method

1. Preheat the oven to 170°C/325°F/Gas Mark 3.
2. Mix the breadcrumbs and oat flakes in a bowl. Whisk the egg in a separate bowl.
3. Dip each strip of fish in the egg then the breadcrumb and oat mix, until completely covered.
4. Put the oil in a frying pan over a medium heat. Cook the fish fingers on each side until golden. Place them on a baking tray and bake in the oven for 10 minutes.
5. Serve with salad or steamed green vegetables on the side.

Halloumi kebabs

Antioxidant-packed vegetables plus delicious protein in the form of halloumi cheese. Children love to assemble these kebabs, as well as to eat them.

Ingredients
300g halloumi cheese, cut into squares
4 small courgettes, cut into thick slices
8 cherry tomatoes
2 tbsp olive oil
Juice and zest of 1 lemon
Salad, to serve

Method
1. If using wooden skewers, soak them in water for 30 minutes before cooking.
2. Thread the halloumi, courgette and cherry tomatoes alternately onto skewers.
3. Cook the kebabs under a hot grill or on a griddle pan for 6-8 minutes, turning occasionally.
4. Meanwhile, whisk together the oil, lemon juice and zest.
5. Drizzle the kebabs with the lemon dressing and serve with salad.

Summing Up

▨ A light cooked lunch makes an alternative to sandwiches for your child.

▨ Combining protein with carbohydrates means energy is released more slowly.

▨ Pasta makes a quick, sustaining meal that children love.

▨ Fish is a nutrient-packed alternative to meat.

Chapter Ten

Tasty Family Dinners

Dinner can be an excellent opportunity to eat, relax and enjoy time together as a family. However, it's not always possible to get to the table at the same time. Even if you can't share a meal, try to sit with your child while they eat their dinner. Aim to eat as a family at some point in the week – it doesn't have to be dinner; a weekend lunch or daily breakfast are brilliant times to catch up over a joint enjoyment of food.

Dinner is often the main meal of the day, although it's often better to eat a larger meal at lunch, when our digestion is more active and we are more likely to move around and use the energy in the food we have consumed. Soups are easy to digest and eat when your child is tired in the evening. In fact, they make a good dinner food for all the family, as any nutrients released from the vegetables are retained in the soup stock, providing a nutrient-rich and delicious broth to enjoy.

Leek and Carrot Soup

This makes a sweet and colourful soup that children enjoy.

Serves 4

Ingredients
2 tbsp extra virgin olive oil
6 large carrots, peeled and sliced
3 leeks, sliced
2 sweet potatoes, peeled and chopped
1 litre of water
Pinch of salt
2 tbsp Parmesan cheese, grated

'Pick and mix – add 150g cooked wholegrain rice to the soup to make a more complete meal.'

Method
1. Put the oil in a large saucepan over a medium heat. Add the vegetables and sauté for 5 minutes, until they start to soften.
2. Add the water and salt and simmer the vegetables for around 20 minutes.
3. Whizz the soup in a blender until smooth. Add the grated Parmesan and serve.

Chicken Soup

The garlic and onion in this soup make it a good choice if your child has a cold or respiratory problems.

Serves 4-6

Ingredients
4-6 chicken thighs, skinned
1 carrot, peeled and chopped
2 stalks of celery, chopped
1 small onion, peeled and chopped
3 cloves garlic, chopped
2 litres water
Pinch of salt
200g broccoli or runner beans, cut into pieces

Method
1. Put all the ingredients, except the broccoli or runner beans, in a large saucepan. Bring the liquid to the boil, lower the heat, cover with a lid and simmer for 45 minutes.
2. Remove the chicken thighs from the soup with a slotted spoon. Pull the meat away from the bones. Chop the meat into pieces and return to the pan.
3. Add the broccoli or runner beans to the soup, heat for 5 minutes, then serve.

Spaghetti with Prawns

Prawns are a good source of omega 3 fatty acids, protein, vitamin B12, zinc and iron. Do not serve them to children younger than five, as they can cause an allergic reaction.

Serves 4-6

Ingredients
6 tbsp extra virgin olive oil
2 cloves garlic, chopped
1 onion, sliced
300g prawns
300g large tomatoes, peeled, seeds removed and chopped
Pinch of salt
2 tbsp fresh parsley, chopped
400g spaghetti

Method
1. Put the oil in a saucepan over a medium heat. Add the garlic and onion and sauté until softened.
2. Add the prawns and cook for 8-10 minutes.
3. Add the tomatoes, salt and parsley and cook for 5 minutes, until the sauce has thickened.
4. Meanwhile, cook the spaghetti following the packet instructions. Drain and put in a serving bowl.
5. Add the sauce and mix with the pasta.

Tagliatelle with Trout

Children enjoy the delicate taste of this fish, which is rich in essential fatty acids.

Ingredients

4 tbsp extra virgin olive oil
1 onion, sliced
2 trout, cleaned, washed and cut into small fillets
200ml vegetable stock
6 large tomatoes, skinned, seeds removed and chopped
3 courgettes, sliced
Pinch of salt
400g egg tagliatelle
2 tbsp fresh parsley, chopped

Method

1. Put the oil in a saucepan over a medium heat. Add the onion and sauté for 5 minutes, until softened.
2. Add the trout fillets, stock, tomatoes, courgettes and salt. Cook gently for 15 minutes until the sauce begins to thicken.
3. Meanwhile, cook the tagliatelle following the packet instructions, then drain and put in a serving bowl.
4. Add the trout sauce, sprinkle with parsley and serve.

'Pick and mix – use fresh tuna as an alternative to trout.'

Ragu

This meat and tomato sauce is a great freezer standby and can be used on any type of pasta, lasagne or gnocchi.

Serves 4-6

Ingredients
4 tbsp extra virgin olive oil
1 onion, chopped
100g bacon
1 clove garlic, chopped
250g minced beef
2 tins chopped tomatoes
Pinch of salt

Method
1. Put the oil in a saucepan over a medium heat and sauté the onion until softened.
2. Add the bacon and garlic and sauté gently for 3-4 minutes.
3. Add the minced meat and cook over a medium heat until browned, stirring occasionally.
4. Add the tomatoes and a pinch of salt. Cook over a low heat for about 40 minutes, stirring occasionally, until the sauce has thickened.

Hunter's Chicken Stew

A tasty combination of protein and vegetables that children and adults love.

Serves 6

Ingredients
4 tbsp extra virgin olive oil
1 knob of butter
1 medium chicken, cut into pieces and seasoned with salt and pepper
1 garlic clove, chopped
1 onion, chopped
120ml white wine
1 tin of tomatoes
Handful fresh rosemary and parsley, chopped
Mashed potatoes or wholegrain rice, to serve
Steamed leafy green vegetables and carrots, to serve

Method
1. Preheat the oven to 180°C/350°F/Gas Mark 4.
2. Heat the oil and butter in a frying pan, add the chicken pieces and sauté until golden. Remove the chicken and reserve.
3. Add the garlic and onion to the pan and sauté until softened.
4. Return the chicken to the pan with the garlic and onions over a medium heat. Pour over the wine and stir until evaporated.
5. Add the tomatoes and herbs to the chicken and transfer to an ovenproof dish.
6. Bake for an hour, or until the chicken is well cooked. Stick the point of a knife into a chicken piece to check the meat is cooked through and the juices are clear.
7. Serve with potatoes or rice and vegetables.

Home-made Pizza

Children enjoy kneading and shaping the pizza dough and choosing their own toppings from a healthy selection.

Serves 6-8

Ingredients

For the dough:
500g strong white bread flour, plus extra for dusting
1 tsp salt
½ tsp sugar
7g sachet of dried yeast
325ml warm water
1 tbsp extra virgin olive oil

For the topping:
200ml jar of passata (pulped tomatoes)
Plus the toppings of your choice

'Pick and mix – try different combinations of toppings, such as spinach and egg; tomato, olive and mozzarella; courgette, aubergine and olive; and ham and ricotta.'

Method

1. Mix the flour, salt, sugar and yeast in a bowl. Add the water and olive oil and mix to form a sticky dough.
2. Turn out the dough onto a floured surface. Knead for around 10 minutes, until the dough is soft and springy.
3. Shape the dough into a round ball, place it in a clean bowl and cover with a plastic bag or a loose layer of cling film. Leave to rise until doubled in size, around 15-20 minutes.
4. Preheat the oven to 250°C/480°F/Gas Mark 9.
5. Around half an hour before you're ready to eat, take a piece of dough the size of a lemon. Roll it into a circle and place on a baking sheet. Continue until you have used all your dough (this should be enough to make 6-8 small pizzas).
6. Spread a spoonful of passata onto each base and place your chosen toppings on top. Bake the pizzas for 7-8 minutes, until the bases are starting to brown and the cheese is bubbling. Serve immediately.

Haddock Gratin

This makes an inexpensive and quick alternative to fish pie.

Ingredients
1.5kg undyed haddock fillets
500ml milk
500ml water
500g broccoli, steamed
60ml crème fraîche or double cream
4 tbsp wholemeal breadcrumbs
Cooked wholegrain rice or wholegrain bread, to serve

Method
1. Preheat the oven to 200°C/400°F/Gas Mark 6.
2. Remove any bones from the fish. Put the fillets in a shallow pan and cover with the milk and water. Put the pan over a high heat and bring the liquid to the boil. Lower the heat and simmer the fish for 5-10 minutes, until cooked
   through and tender. Remove fish from the cooking liquid.
3. Remove the skin and flake the fish into a shallow baking dish with the steamed broccoli. Pour over the crème fraîche or cream and sprinkle over the breadcrumbs.
4. Bake for 25 minutes, until bubbling. Serve with wholegrain rice or chunks of wholegrain bread.

'Pick and mix – use unsmoked fish, such as salmon and cod and swap spinach or shredded cabbage for the broccoli.'

Creamy Risotto

This dish is high in vitamins, so it's perfect for boosting a young or weak immune system. It's also easy to make and your child will love creating the vegetable decorations around the side of the plate.

Serves 4

Ingredients
350g risotto rice
2 carrots
150g peas
100g Brussels sprouts or runner beans
1 tbsp extra virgin olive oil, plus extra for drizzling
1 onion, chopped
1 clove garlic, chopped
1 stick celery, finely chopped
240ml passata
Salt and freshly ground black pepper
240ml single cream

Method
1. Boil the rice in water for 30-40 minutes until tender, or according to the packet instructions.
2. Steam the carrots, peas and Brussels sprouts or runner beans until tender. When cooked, chop the carrots into cubes. Reserve the vegetables.
3. Put the olive oil in a small saucepan over a medium heat. Add the onion, garlic and celery and sauté for 3-4 minutes, until softened. Add the passata and seasoning, and cook for about 15 minutes. Add boiled water to thin the sauce, if necessary.
4. Whiz the sauce in a blender and stir in the cream. Return the sauce to the saucepan and warm through for 2-3 minutes.
5. Place the rice in a dish and stir in two-thirds of the vegetables. Drizzle with olive oil.
6. Use the remaining vegetables to decorate around the sides of the dish and serve with the sauce on the side.

Mackerel Fish Cakes

Mackerel contains essential fatty acids that will help your child's brain development. These make a great alternative to traditional beef burgers.

Ingredients
250g cooked mackerel fillets
175g potato, cooked and mashed
25g butter, melted
4 tbsp extra virgin olive oil or more if needed
2 spring onions, chopped
1 tbsp milk
1 tbsp oatmeal
Wholegrain bread rolls and sliced tomatoes, to serve

Method
1. Remove the skin and any bones from the mackerel fillets. Mash them with a fork in a bowl and mix in the mashed potato and melted butter.
2. Put 1 tbsp olive oil in a saucepan over a medium heat. Add the spring onion and sauté for 3 minutes, until softened. Stir the spring onion into the fish and potato mix. If the mixture is very stiff, add a little milk to loosen.
3. Shape the mixture into fish cakes, then put into the fridge to chill for at least 30 minutes.
4. Dust the fish cakes on both sides with oatmeal. Put the remaining oil in the frying pan over a medium heat. Fry the fish cakes in batches until golden on both sides. Drain on kitchen paper.
5. Serve in wholemeal buns with slices of tomato.

'Pick and mix – use tinned salmon or tuna as an alternative to mackerel.'

Summing Up

- Try to eat dinner together as a family as often as possible. If that's not possible, sit at the table with your child as they eat.

- It's often better to have a larger lunch than dinner.

- Soups make an easy-to-digest, nutrient-rich dinner choice.

- Choose meals your child can help to make, such as pizza or risotto.

- Make extra quantities of ragu and soup, so you can freeze some for another day.

Chapter Eleven

Snacks and Treats

Children have small stomachs and a lot of energy, so between-meal snacks can provide the extra calories and goodness they need to keep them on the go. The right snack foods also help to balance blood sugar levels, reducing mood swings and irritability. Unless there is a medical reason not to, giving your child the occasional treat is absolutely fine.

What won't work is giving so many snacks that they won't eat their proper meals. Providing home-made snacks and treats, rather than bought and processed ones, will also help your child to grow accustomed to healthier options. Take a look at the recipes below, plus see chapter 5 for other fast snack ideas.

'Pick and mix – try crushed blueberries or raspberries instead of strawberries.'

Strawberry Fool

A great alternative to bought flavoured yoghurts. Avoid using honey if your child is under one.

Serves 4

Ingredients
400g strawberries, hulled (stems cut out) and crushed, plus extra to decorate
450g thick Greek yoghurt
2 tsp honey

Method
1. Stir the the strawberries, yoghurt and honey gently together, to create a swirl of pink and white.
2. Spoon into bowls, decorate with a strawberry and serve.

Alternative Oven Chips

Chips are loved by every child. These oven-cooked potatoes have the same great taste but are low in fat and rich in fibre and vitamin C.

Serves 3-4

Ingredients
2 tbsp olive oil
1 clove garlic, mashed
400g large potatoes, scrubbed
Salt (optional)

Method
1. Mix the garlic with the olive oil.
2. Slice the potatoes lengthwise in large segments.
3. Place the potatoes on a nonstick oven tray. Sprinkle with the oil and garlic mixture and add a pinch of salt (optional).
4. Bake for 30 minutes, or until the potatoes are golden brown and cooked through.

Potato Croquettes

A great combination of carbohydrate from the potatoes and protein from the cheese. Delicious eaten warm or cold.

Makes 12-15 croquettes

Ingredients
600g potatoes
1 egg yolk
50g pecorino cheese
50g Parmesan cheese
1 tbsp fresh parsley, chopped

For the coating:
Plain flour, for dusting
1 egg, beaten
3 slices wholemeal bread, whizzed into breadcrumbs
Extra virgin olive oil, for frying

Method
1. Put the unpeeled potatoes in a saucepan, cover with water, and boil over a high heat until tender. Leave to cool.
2. Peel then mash the potatoes. Stir in the egg yolk, pecorino cheese, Parmesan cheese and parsley.
3. Roll the mixture into sausage shapes and put them in the fridge for at least 20 minutes, to firm up.
4. Roll the croquettes in the flour to coat lightly, dip into the beaten egg and then roll in the breadcrumbs.
5. Heat the olive oil in a saucepan over a medium heat. Fry the croquettes until golden, drain on kitchen paper and serve.

Home-made Hummus

Hummus, made from chickpeas and tahini paste, is a good source of vitamins and energy.

Ingredients
1 tin chickpeas, drained (reserve 2-3 tbsp water from the tin)
3 tbsp tahini
1 or 2 cloves garlic, crushed
3 tbsp extra virgin olive oil
Pinch of sea salt
3 tbsp lemon juice
1 tbsp fresh mint or parsley, chopped

Method
1. Put the chickpeas, tahini and garlic in a blender and whiz into a smooth paste. If the paste is too stiff, add a little of the water to loosen.
2. Put the chickpea paste in a bowl and stir in the olive oil, salt, lemon juice and herbs. The hummus will keep in the fridge for a week.

Carrot biscuits

Carrots give these nutty biscuits a naturally sweet taste – a tasty alternative to carrot cake and will stay fresh for around a week.

Makes 10 biscuits

Ingredients

120g carrots, chopped
1 egg, whisked
2 tbsp milk
4 tsp clear honey
50g butter, softened
100g plain flour
Half 7g sachet dried yeast
50g walnuts, chopped
2oz raisins

Method

1. Preheat the oven to 180°C/350°F/Gas Mark 4.
2. Cook the carrots in boiling water until soft. Drain and mash.
3. When the carrots are cold, mix them with the egg, milk, honey and butter. Stir in the flour, yeast, walnuts and raisins.
4. Place spoonfuls of mixture onto a baking tray and bake for 15-20 minutes, until golden.

Baked Apples

A delicious afternoon snack or pudding, made with vitamin-rich fresh and dried fruit.

Ingredients
50g raisins
4 tsp honey
1 tsp cinnamon
4 medium cooking apples, cores removed

Method
1. Preheat the oven to 190°C/375°F/Gas Mark 5.
2. In a bowl, mix together the raisins, honey and cinnamon.
3. Fill the apples with the raisin mixture and place in a shallow baking dish.
4. Pour 2 tbsp hot water around the apples and bake for 30 minutes, or until soft. Serve warm or cold.

Chocolate Mousse

Serves 4

Ingredients
120 g plain chocolate, broken into small pieces)
1 tbsp milk
3 eggs, separated
30g butter
50g white chocolate, grated

Method
1. Place the plain chocolate and milk in bowl over a pan of simmering water. Stir until the chocolate has completely melted. Take care not to overheat.
2. Beat together the egg yolks and the butter until smooth.
3. Add the yolk mixture to the melted chocolate, stirring vigorously with a wooden spoon, then remove from the heat.
4. Whisk the egg white until stiff. Fold a spoonful into the chocolate mixture; when incorporated, gently fold in the rest of the egg whites.
5. Pour the mixture into serving bowl and chill for two hours or so.
6. Sprinkle the white chocolate over the top and serve.

Pear Tart

A small slice of this will satisfy your child. Keep the tart in an airtight tin, where it will stay fresh for three or four days.

Ingredients
3 eggs
150g sugar
100g butter, softened
3 tbsp milk, warmed
100g white plain flour
100g wholemeal plain flour
Half 7g sachet dried yeast
200g pears, peeled, cored and sliced
Juice and zest of one lemon

'Pick and mix – use slices of apple, instead of pear, to make the tart filling.'

Method
1. Beat together the eggs and sugar. Add the butter and milk, and beat again.
2. Sift the flour and gradually stir it in to the mixture. Add the yeast and stir again.
3. Grease and flour an ovenproof dish or tart tin. Pour the mixture into the tin and top with the fruit. Bake for 40 minutes, until golden. Serve cold.

Well-Cool Ice Lollies

Children love making their own ice lollies, and with this recipe you can be sure that they're packed with real fruit. You can buy inexpensive lolly kits from supermarkets and cookshops, or make your own from yoghurt pots and saved and washed wooden lolly sticks.

Ingredients
150g caster sugar
300ml water

For the flavourings:
500g fresh strawberries and 50ml lemon juice
Or
300ml freshly squeezed orange juice and 50ml lemon juice

Method
1. Put the caster sugar and water into a saucepan over a low heat. Stir until the sugar has dissolved.
2. Turn up the heat and boil the syrup for 5 minutes. Switch off the heat and leave the syrup to cool.
3. For strawberry lollies, rub the fruit through a sieve to make a purée.
4. Mix the purée and lemon juice with the syrup and pour into your lolly moulds. Or, for orange lollies, mix the orange and lemon juices to the syrup and pour into your lolly moulds.
5. Freeze the lollies until solid. Dip the moulds into warm water to release the lollies.

'Pick and mix – raspberries and blackberries make tasty purées to flavour lollies.'

Summing Up

▓ Healthy snacks can help to balance your child's blood sugar levels throughout the day, providing energy and goodness.

▓ The occasional treat is fine to eat, unless your child has a medical problem.

▓ Making your own snacks and treats can encourage a taste for healthier options in your child.

▓ Bear in mind that constant snacking will reduce your child's appetite for main meals.

Chapter Twelve

'Medicine Cabinet' Meals

A warming meal can be the perfect remedy when your child is feeling poorly. But it's about more than comfort food. The following suggestions are power-packed food 'prescriptions' that may help to boost your child's wellbeing. However, all suggestions made in this chapter are general and not intended to replace medical professional treatment.

Cold and flu

The following foods may help to reduce sniffles and boost the immune system.

- Chicken soup (see recipe, chapter 10) – full of nutrients and with garlic and onion, which can support the respiratory system.

- Sprinkle wheatgerm on salads or breakfast. It's rich in vitamins B and E, zinc, magnesium and iron to boost wellbeing.

- Cow's milk can increase mucus levels, use soya milk as an alternative.

- Give citrus fruit or juice, which is rich in vitamin C and can help to boost immunity

- Carrots and dark green vegetables offer a good source of vitamin C, zinc and beta carotene, which is converted to vitamin A in the body. All of these nutrients can help to support the immune system.

- Garlic has antibacterial properties and can be added to many different meals.

- Manuka honey contains tea tree pollen, which can help to reduce sinus congestion. Make a warm drink for your child with hot water, 1 tsp Manuka honey and a slice of lemon. But do not give honey if your child is under one.

Nosebleeds

Recurrent nosebleeds can be very common in children. Your child may also experience nosebleeds during a cold, when the nasal membrane is more delicate than normal and nose blowing can damage the blood vessels.

▨ Green vegetables contain vitamin K, which is beneficial for blood clotting, and vitamin C to help strengthen the capillaries.

▨ However, consult a GP if you are worried about your child's nosebleeds.

Eczema

This itchy skin condition can be distressing for children.

▨ Alternate daily juices of freshly squeezed carrots, mangoes or papayas, which are rich in skin-supporting beta carotene and antioxidants.

Acne

A diet rich in omega 3 foods may help to alleviate skin problems (see chapter 2).

▨ Salmon, sardines, fresh tuna and other oily fish are rich in omega 3 essential fatty acids.

▨ Seeds such as flaxseed, pumpkin and walnuts are also rich in omega 3 – sprinkle them on breakfast cereals and salads, or give to your child as a tasty snack.

▨ Dark green, leafy vegetables contain omega 3.

▨ Choose foods that are rich in fibre, such as wholegrain bread and fruit.

▨ Serve soups such as minestrone – they're rich in vitamins and minerals that support the skin.

▨ Zinc-rich foods, such as fish, lean red meat, poultry, dairy products, wholegrain rice and nuts and seeds are important for healthy skin, especially during puberty.

▨ Cut down your child's intake of simple carbohydrates, fried and processed foods – the reduction in salt and sugar will support skin health.

Cold sores

Arginine is an amino acid that can worsen the symptoms of cold sores. It is found in foods such as wheat cereals, peanuts, almonds, chocolate and bacon. However lysine, another amino acid, may inhibit the cold sore virus. By increasing your child's intake of lysine-rich foods and avoiding those that contain arginine, you may reduce the occurrence of cold sores.

- Cut back on peanut butter, white flour products, fried foods, butter, nuts and seeds and chocolate, which contain arginine.
- Lysine-rich foods include fish, red meat, chicken and turkey, watercress and beans.
- Eggs, dairy products and soya foods also contain high levels of lysine.

Earache

Certain foods seem to increase the production of mucus in some people. If your child has an earache, it may be worth avoiding these. Always consult a GP if you are worried about your child's ear pain.

- Maximise your child's intake of antioxidants by serving lots of fresh fruit and vegetables.
- Avoid dairy products and fatty foods, as these may cause excess mucus production.
- Give your child water, rather than fruit juices (apart from pineapple) or sugary drinks. The sugars can feed the bacteria causing the problem.
- Pineapple juice may help to thin the secretion of mucus.

Anaemia

Iron-rich foods can help to boost levels of this essential mineral in the body.

- Give your child figs, brown rice, beets, poultry, eggs and raisins.
- Include plenty of green, leafy vegetables. These contain vitamin C, which aids iron absorption.

Instant Energising Soup

This raw 'soup' is an ideal pick-me-up when your child is feeling poorly, or to boost their energy after illness.

Serves 3-4

Ingredients
3 carrots, peeled and sliced
1 stick celery, sliced
Handful mixed green tender salad leaves
125g fresh green peas
1 tbsp mixed sesame and sunflower seeds
425ml water
1 papaya, mango or avocado

Method
1. Whizz the carrots, celery, salad leaves, peas, seeds and water in a blender, until smooth.
2. Add the papaya, mango or avocado and blend again. Chill and serve.

Immunity-booster Soup

Tasty, easy to digest and packed with vitamins, this soup is a great option when your child is feeling poorly.

Serves 4

Ingredients
4 carrots, diced
2 unpeeled sweet potatoes, chopped
1 potato, peeled and diced
½ bulb fennel, chopped
1 onion, peeled and sliced
3 sticks celery, sliced
2 tbsp fresh parsley, chopped
200g broccoli or cabbage, chopped
425ml water or vegetable stock
1 tsp miso (a traditional Japanese seasoning)

Method
1. Put all the ingredients, except the miso, in a saucepan over a medium heat and simmer for 40-60 minutes.
2. For a thick soup, whiz in a blender until smooth and serve. For a lighter option, strain the soup, reserving the broth and discarding the vegetables.
3. Stir the miso into the soup and serve.

Summing Up

- Well-chosen meals can provide comfort and essential nutrients when your child is ill.

- Foods that reduce mucus production and boost immunity may help recovery from cold and flu.

- Vitamins K and C may help to reduce nosebleeds.

- Beta carotene-rich foods may soothe eczema.

- Omega 3 essential oils can help to support skin health in children with acne.

- Reducing intake of arginine-rich foods and boosting lysine-rich foods in the diet may help to reduce occurrence of cold sores.

- Cutting back on sugar and mucus-forming foods may help in cases of earache.

- Foods high in iron are beneficial for anaemic conditions.

- Soups are high in nutrients and easy for your child to eat when they are feeling ill.

Help List

If you have any concerns about your child's health or their diet, contact your child's GP or paediatrician. The following organisations may also provide helpful advice and products. The contact details were correct at the time of publication.

Food and nutrition information and support

British Association for Nutritional Therapists (BANT)

www.bant.org.uk
The professional body for nutritional therapists, the website has a register of practitioners.

British Nutrition Foundation (BNF)

www.nutrition.org.uk
Delivers evidence-based information on food and nutrition in the context of health and lifestyle.

The Food Commission

www.foodcomm.org.uk
www.chewonthis.org.uk
Independent food watchdog. The Chew On This website has been created for children aged 11 to 14 to teach them about food production and the importance of good nutrition for wellbeing.

Food Standards Agency (FSA)

www.food.gov.uk
www.eatwell.gov.uk
Latest news and guidelines on a range of food issues, including labelling, allergies and food safety.

The Nutri Centre

enq@nutricentre.com

www.nutricentre.com

Offers advice on nutrition and sells a range of nutritional supplements.

The Vegan Society

www.vegansociety.com

Educational charity providing guidance on veganism, including information on raising infants and children on a vegan diet, soya infant formula, and baby and toddler recipes.

Vegetarian Society

www.vegsoc.org

Information for anyone following a meat-free diet, including a dedicated section for 'Young Veggies'.

Health and wellbeing information and support

British Heart Foundation

www.bhf.org.uk

Research and campaign charity dedicated to improving heart health. Runs the Food4Thought initiative to tackle childhood obesity through diet and activity, and is campaigning for clearer food labelling.

Department of Health

www.dh.gov.uk

Information on government health targets, plus guidance on obesity and nutritional programmes.

Homeopathic Medical Association

www.the-hma.org

Register of qualified professional homeopaths, plus information on using homeopathy.

NHS Choices

www.nhs.uk
A huge range of information on nutrition and lifestyle, including Live Well,
Healthier Shopping and Health A-Z sections.

NHS Direct

Tel: 0845 4647
www.nhsdirect.nhs.uk
A 24-hour healthcare service via telephone and email, plus online nutrition
information.

Allergy information and support

Allergy UK

www.allergyuk.org
www.foodintoleranceawareness.org
www.blossomcampaign.org
The UK's leading medical charity dealing with allergies. Offers a helpline, plus
food alerts and a list of approved products. Its Blossom Campaign provides
advice on childhood allergy.

Eating disorders information and support

Anorexia and Bulimia Care (ABC)

Tel: 01934 710 679 (sufferer's helpline)
01934 710 645 (parent helpine)
www.anorexiabulimiacare.co.uk
Advice and support for people with eating disorders and their families.

BEAT (Beating Eating Disorders)

www.b-eat.co.uk
The leading UK charity for people with eating disorders and their families.

Obesity information and support

Association for the Study of Obesity

www.aso.org.uk
UK's leading charity dedicated to understanding and treating obesity.

MEND

www.mendcentral.org
MEND (Mind, Exercise, Nutrition ... Do it!) is a social programme dedicated to reducing obesity levels and helping children and their families to become fitter, healthier and happier. Organises free healthy living programmes in the community and has joined with National Obesity Forum to launch National Childhood Obesity Week.

National Obesity Forum

www.nationalobesityforum.org.uk
Raises awareness of impact of obesity on health. Includes information for children and families.

Hyperactivity information and support

Hyperactive Children's Support Group (HACSG)

www.hacsg.org.uk
Support group offering dietary approach to the problem of hyperactivity.

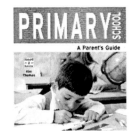

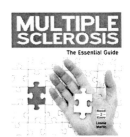

Peppa Meets The Queen

Peppa and her family are watching television.
Suddenly, there is a special announcement
from the Queen.